The SUMMER GARDEN

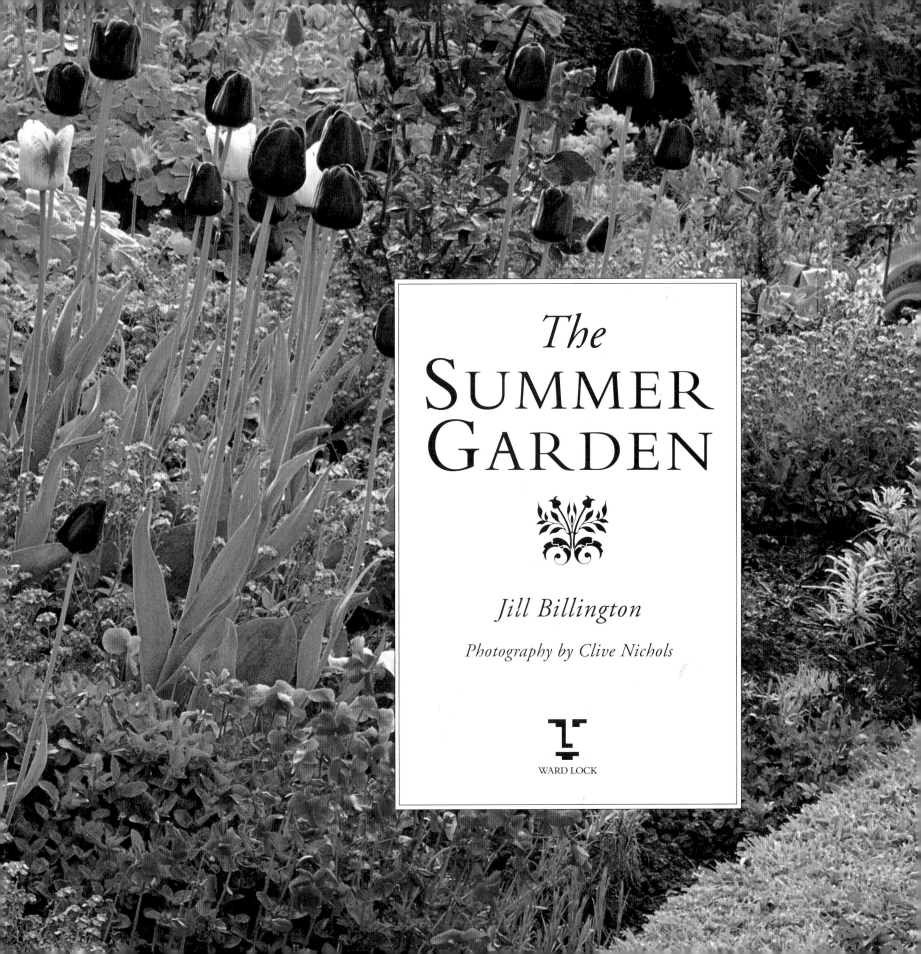

The SUMMER GARDEN

Jill Billington

Photography by Clive Nichols

WARD LOCK

Dedication

To my parents, Walter and Lilian Annis, who both love gardens

A WARD LOCK BOOK
First published in the UK 1997 by Ward Lock
Wellington House, 125 Strand
LONDON WC2R 0BB

A Cassell Imprint

Distributed in the United States by Sterling Publishing Co., Inc.
387 Park Avenue South, New York, NY 10016–8810

A British Library Cataloguing in Publication Data block for this book may be obtained from the British Library

ISBN 0 7063 7455 X

Designed by Richard Carr
Printed and bound in Spain

Page 1
A detail of Allium christophii.

Page 2/3
Late-flowering tulips 'Queen of Night' and 'Magier' above a sea of Myosotis *'Blue Ball'.*

Page 5 (top)
Agapanthus *Headbourne Hybrids,* Salvia patens, Anthemis tinctoria *'E.C. Buxton' and* Tropaeolum majus *'Empress of India'.*

Page 5 (below)
Long after it has flowered, Malus floribunda *is notable again, encircled by oriental poppies.*

CONTENTS

INTRODUCTION

Symmetrical planting of clipped box and the unusual Salix integra *'Hakuro-nishiki', framed overhead by* Rosa *'Rambling Rector', are contained by the low edging of* Lavandula angustifolia *'Hidcote'.*

The sumptuous beauty of the summer garden, when constantly changing colours and patterns stir the senses, is the subject of this book. Most gardeners realize that there is more to creating a garden than a love of plants. We have all indulged ourselves in garden centres, finding a plant so irresistible that we bring it home to plant out – but where is it to go?

I stress throughout the importance of a unified design, both in the layout of the garden and in the planting. I show how plants may be chosen to make a permanent three-dimensional framework for the garden plan, where spaces are enclosed and the eye is directed towards open views or hidden areas. Attention is drawn to the natural shapes and habits of plants as well as to their colour and

texture, as it is by such means that successful schemes are made.

Creating gardens is an art form that has followed the twists and turns of fashion over the centuries in the pursuit of beauty. Now opportunities are far broader than in the past. Plants are available from all over the world, and choices are magnified many times by the work of the hybridists. For summer the options are even greater, which is very exciting but can be bewildering. It is the aim of this book to clarify the choices and show how to use them, describing plants which, beautiful in their own right, nevertheless have a larger role to play as part of the theatre of summer.

Summer is the bounteous season, desired and held in the memory. Yet gardens should be attractive at other times of the year, so the book begins by outlining the principles of designing the garden as a whole. The summer garden is prepared for in winter, when there is time to consider what is wanted and how to achieve it. The growing season follows through the freshness of spring, until it reaches the summer zenith, with its colour, scents and humming movement. Then come the changing harmonies of late summer as it passes on to the final vibrancy of the fall.

Good planning is concerned with function as well as beauty. As part of the preparations, horticultural details are included on how to achieve the summer radiance; planting techniques and soils being as important as the aesthetic concerns of designing.

The first two chapters describe trees and shrubs that will provide the solid forms and masses of the garden plan. These also create links through to the other seasons, either as evergreens, as distinctive shapes or by their foliage, flowers and fruit.

Summer means different things to different people and to many, summer spells roses. Therefore, I have given them a chapter of their own. This describes the different types of roses and suggests how they are used in varied styles of garden. Plant associates that work particularly well are included.

To others, the essence of summer is the 'careless rapture' of the herbaceous border, with its colour and shapeliness lasting for months and constantly changing. The chapter on the uses of perennials in flowering sequence forms the main focus of the book. I have divided the summer period into early, mid- and late summer, in each case tracing how one flower group gives way to another as each reaches its peak.

Not everyone has the space or time for large borders. Some of us have only small backyards with little planting space, while for others the climate may be unsuitable for a huge range of perennial flowers. I have therefore included a chapter on the annual garden, in which plants may be grown for the summer season alone. In this chapter there are also ideas for using tender or exotic plants in summer containers.

Another chapter is devoted to the use of plants in different aspects in the garden. For example, one area might be permanently shaded and damp. And since, in the hazy heat of summer days there is charm in providing cool, shaded retreats, I discuss plants that are suited to shade. Many subtly coloured plants, and some particularly well-foliaged ones, flourish in dappled shade, especially in damp conditions. There are also plants that are adapted to the dryness of sunny exposed sites. Among these, many of the grey-leaved plants, exotics and succulents do very well. By selecting the right plant for specific conditions, the gardener will be saved the disappointment and expense of failure.

A chapter on herbs is included for those of a nostalgic turn of mind or for those whose enthusiasm for herbs lies in their culinary and medicinal uses. But it is the inherent charm of herbs with which the chapter is mainly concerned – with the subtle beauty of their soft colours, richly varied textures and aromatic foliage, which add piquancy to the summer season.

Redolent of high summer, the lush flowers of Campanula lactiflora *'Prichard's Variety' dominate the low Shrub roses and edging lavender.*

I also draw attention to grasses, whose floating flowers and swaying leaves form an intrinsic part of the spirit of summer. A chapter is devoted to this style of gardening, for grasses are decorative for many months, not only when they are in flower.

From all these options, the reader will be able to identify what is required for his or her own garden.

The plant profiles at the end of the book will help you in your choice of plants, but do indulge your personal passions and enjoy also the gifts of friends. No garden should exclude individual enthusiasm; it is the personal touch that turns a bland garden into something beautiful and out of the ordinary.

1 • PREPARING FOR SUMMER

The quiet time, when the last flash of autumn is over and domestic life resumes indoors, is when planning starts in earnest. Summer gardens are all about plants and how we design with them, but to be sure of success, planning and preparation do need careful attention. A good basic plan should enhance the flowers of summer.

WHAT DO YOU HAVE?

Initially you must assess what you already have, good or bad. Many of us inherit established gardens, so look afresh and decide whether it works for you.

It is worth sketching a scaled diagram, similar to that shown in Fig. 1 (below). This will help you evaluate your site, to see where the summer emphasis will be. The essential considerations are:

1 Where are the boundaries and what are they?

Do you have hedges, walls, fences?
Are they in good condition?

2 Sketch in the main house as it relates to the garden.

Where is the access?
Are there French doors?
Is there a conservatory?
Where is the kitchen door?
Where are the windows and are the views important?
Are there other buildings like a shed or summer house?
Is there an oil tank or any other fixed feature?

Steps lead through to a garden of pinks, blues, lilac and purple. The flowers are erigeron, lathyrus, geraniums and diascia.

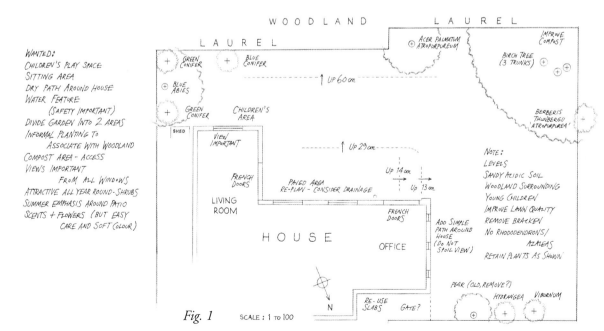

WANTED:
CHILDREN'S PLAY SPACE
SITTING AREA
DRY PATH AROUND HOUSE
WATER FEATURE
    (SAFETY IMPORTANT)
DIVIDE GARDEN INTO 2 AREAS
INFORMAL PLANTING TO
    ASSOCIATE WITH WOODLAND
COMPOST AREA - ACCESS
VIEWS IMPORTANT
    FROM ALL WINDOWS
ATTRACTIVE ALL YEAR ROUND-SHRUBS
SUMMER EMPHASIS AROUND PATIO
SCENTS + FLOWERS (BUT EASY
    CARE AND SOFT COLOUR)

Fig. 1   SCALE : 1 TO 100

This elegant town garden shows how effective a symmetrical design can be in a small space.

3 Check the aspect of the garden.

Where is north?
Do adjacent buildings or trees shade the garden?

4 Miscellaneous features.

Retain access to man-hole covers.
Look for overhead cables.

5 Is the land level?

Do you have a gentle slope?
Would you prefer to level it?
Is terracing necessary?

6 What are your surroundings?

Are you overlooked?
Are you surrounded by fields?
Is there a pleasant view?
Is there an ugly view?

7 What is your climate?

Is local weather significant?
What is the depth of winter frost?
Do you have excessive summer heat?
Is drought likely?

8 Is your garden exposed or protected?

Is it in a town?
Is it enclosed and inward looking?
Is it a country garden?
Is it exposed to wind?

9 What existing plants are there?

Are there mature trees?
Are there mature shrubs?
Are there existing hedges?
Are any of the above worth keeping?
What should go?
Are there summer climbers?

Is there a kitchen garden?

Are there herbaceous plants that you would like to keep?

(A temporary 'nursery bed' could be provided to save any special plants.)

10 Soil quality must be assessed.

What is the physical condition?

Is it acidic or alkaline?

Has the top soil been stripped leaving only subsoil?

Is the site properly drained?

Once these questions have been answered, turn your attention to your personal goals for a summer garden.

WHAT DO YOU WANT?

Write a list of your aims as these will affect the end result, as can be seen in Fig. 2 (below). The following list suggests what some of these aims may be.

1 Use of the garden

Privacy for outdoor living

Family recreation

Entertaining – barbecues, seats, tables

Growing fresh food

Horticultural interest

2 Solutions to problems

Does drainage need sorting out first?

Do the levels need attention?

Is it worth putting in an irrigation system?

Should you provide a windbreak?

Does the soil need thorough conditioning?

3 Features in the garden

Terrace or patio

Lawn for recreational games

Lawn with planted beds

Steps, paths and raised beds

Pond, fountain or swimming pool

Summer house, pergola, arbour

Service area

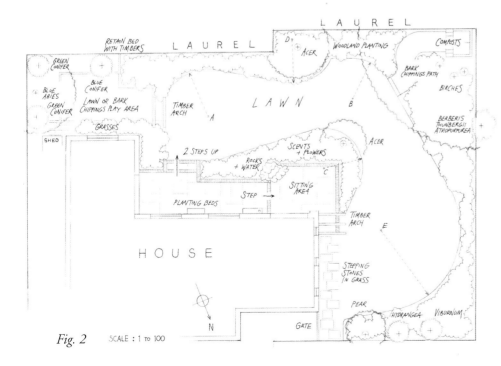

Fig. 2   SCALE : 1 to 100

4 What style of garden would you like?

Geometric and formal garden (box hedging, pergolas, rose gardens, herb gardens)
Romantic and informal garden (mixed herbaceous garden, rustic arbours and winding paths)
Country garden (orchards, grasses, flowers)
Sophisticated garden (elegant furniture, formal entertaining)

HOW TO DEVISE THE LAYOUT

Having established what you have and what you want, the next step is concerned with layout. Simple layouts are most effective. Let the plants themselves be the centre of attention without having to compete with an over-fussy planting plan.

Spaces

Spaces are important as a balance to the luxuriant mass of summer plants. There is nothing so tranquil as a stretch of green lawn. Alternatively, paving or gravel may be used to provide spacious, uncluttered areas. The aim is always to provide a foil for the glories of summer flowers.

Materials

For the same reason, when you are choosing materials, whether flagstones, bricks, concrete or timber, stick to one type, or at most two types, without excessive contrast of colour or fussy patterns.

All-over texture, like that of small unit paving of setts, bricks or cobbles, will work well as long as the pattern is uncomplicated.

Hard surfaces such as stone contrast with the fragility of plant material. Timber decking, on the other hand, blends harmoniously.

Opposite: A tranquil area is created by placing a swinging seat among summer plants.

Seating areas

A paved area near the house should be comfortably spaced for chairs. If the sunnier part of the garden is away from the house, create a paved area there, which can be reached by a path.

Provide shaded or 'secret' places to sit – for example, a seat beneath a tree. This is a great benefit in hot climates.

Focal points and views

There should also be spaces to 'rest' the eye. Accents might be a summer house, a sculpture, an urn or simply a particularly well-planned plant group or a tree.

Views from the house will include such accents. They may also suggest hidden delights. The whole garden need not be immediately visible. Plan small garden rooms, such as rose gardens, or devise paths that lead out of sight.

Paths

I have strong views about paths. Obviously they provide dry-footed access all year round and must be practical, ideally allowing two people to walk side by side. An ideal width is 1.2m (4ft) or more, and the narrowest is 1m (3ft).

Above all, however, paths must lead somewhere. If they are straight they should lead to a gate, seat, service area or a building, not leave you stranded. If they are curved, they must lead around something, say a tree or shrub. A winding path that meanders purposelessly looks fussy, but if it curves around a summer border, enabling you to study the display, it is more charming.

HOW TO ACHIEVE SUCCESS

Having resolved the overall garden design, consider the essentials of soil preparation.

Soil

It is important to understand the nature of your soil. The physical structure of the soil is complex. It can vary from free-draining sand (through which water drains quickly, taking the nutrients with it) to heavy, compacted clay (which can 'drown' the fibrous roots of some plants, depriving them of oxygen).

You need to know whether your soil is acid, alkaline or neutral, for some plants need an acid soil and will fail to thrive or even die in alkaline conditions, whereas others flourish best on chalk or limestone. Simple testing kits, which can be purchased from any garden centre, show the level of acidity on a sliding scale described as pH. A soil that registers below pH 4.5 is extremely acidic, while one that has pH levels towards 8.1 is increasingly alkaline. A level of around 6.5 is mildly acidic and ideal for most plants. Always take a few tests, in different parts of the garden, about 10cm (4in) deep.

I must stress the importance of good planting preparation. Well-worked, aerated and fertile loam that is neither too wet nor too dry is the ideal planting medium.

Winter is the ideal time to dig over the soil for the herbaceous beds. The first aim is to improve the physical structure by incorporating bulky rotted humus. This will help to retain nutrients and moisture in sandy soils and to break up the heavy consistency of clay soils. Heavy clods of clay, if exposed to frost, will form a more manageable soil by spring.

To improve fertility, add organic or synthetic fertilizers. The first are derived from natural materials including bonemeal, hoof and horn meal, fish, blood and bone. Proprietary manufactured fertilizers are efficiently balanced and often easy to distribute.

Planting

Having prepared the soil in winter, most planting starts in spring after the soil has warmed up. You could have planted bare-rooted trees and shrubs in the previous autumn, which is the ideal time, but many trees and shrubs are now available in containers, and these may be put in later as long as the soil is neither frozen nor water-logged.

Dig a deeper and wider hole than the container or root system of the plant, pierce the sides of the hole with a fork, incorporate enriched peat, or a substitute, with some rotted organic matter and add a 'slow-release' or proprietary fertilizer. Soak containerized and bare-rooted plants in water for at least an hour before planting, and be sure that they are planted at the same depth to which they have become accustomed. Tease out the roots and fill in with topsoil and/or compost, making sure that roots are all in contact with the soil and that there are no pockets of air. Then firm in carefully and water thoroughly after planting.

Maturity in the garden

If your garden contains old established trees and shrubs you will probably wish to retain them. However, if the garden is brand new, you will be able to watch the young garden as it matures.

Shrubs and trees obviously take a considerable time to become established, although you can buy large specimen plants, already grown on by the nursery. These will define the design framework very quickly, although their growth will be checked by transplanting. A word of warning: wind is the enemy of large specimens when their roots are not firmly in the soil, and careful staking and even guys may be necessary.

Herbaceous plants do become established much more quickly. In the first year they will attain height but no real width, so fill the gaps with annuals, either sown from seed or as bedding plants, as described on pages 82–95.

By the third year, the herbaceous perennials will be looking very good indeed and will distract attention from the youth of the shrubs. Soon, some of the herbaceous plants will need splitting and re-planting.

By the fifth year, most of the shrubs will be providing a solid framework for the design. They will need pruning to keep them in shape, and hedging will need regular clipping. The tree canopies will develop, changing the light beneath and resulting in a few planting adaptations.

In ten years the garden will have achieved a look of maturity in summer as the garden-sized trees will have developed thick trunks and wide canopies. Many of the perennials will have been thinned.

The speed of growth varies widely from genus to genus, and even from species to species. Herbaceous plants particularly need continuous revision. Some live for years, spreading and possibly covering adjacent plants. Others are shorter lived but will scatter their seeds widely. Often such re-distribution adds new design ideas, and the garden will look different year by year. This is one of the greatest charms of the summer garden.

Rosa 'Bobbie James' and lavatera frame the entrance to a richly planted herbaceous garden.

2 · TREES GIVE HEIGHT

The wide-spreading Catalpa bignonioides *'Aurea' dominates a yellow, blue and silver planting scheme.*

Few gardens are complete without trees. They form important elements of any garden design and are among the first planting priorities. Trees are a part of our horizons, both literally and by aspiration. They are looked up to, venerated for their age and appreciated for their gifts. We like to have them around.

You may already have trees in your garden that you can work into your plan. If not, the choice and siting of new trees will demand careful consideration. Your decisions about both species and position will be influenced not only by the size of your garden but also by its soil type and its micro-climate.

Richly red and orange, the textured foliage of the sweet gum, Liquidambar styraciflua, *is famous for its fiery end to summer.*

Trees need careful siting. Some trees, like the lovely, densely leaved *Cercidiphyllum japonicum,* need rich, deep soil that does not dry out, while others, like the more tender silver *Acacia dealbata* (silver wattle or mimosa tree), with its feathery leaves and powdery gold flowers, thrive in sandy soil.

Wind can also be a problem. Some trees – silver birches, hazels, hornbeams, hawthorns, rowans, ash and beech, for example – can cope with cold exposed situations. Some, like *Crataegus laevigata* (hawthorn), *Fraxinus ornus* (manna ash), the autumn-colouring *Liquidambar styraciflua,* the amelanchier and the willows, benefit from damp soils. Others, such as the birches, most hawthorns, prunus, ash, catalpa, ginkgo and crabapples, will cope with pollution. Trees, such as the acers, crabapples, hornbeams, laburnum, flowering cherries and rowans, will tolerate heavy clay soils. Although you will initially be choosing plants for aesthetic reasons, do always check their horticultural strengths as well.

The ultimate height and spread are also important. Trees like birches, rowans or aspens may be quite closely planted, as little as 2m (7ft) apart, and it is worth remembering that grouping uneven numbers is usually more aesthetically pleasing than even numbers. Trees that are grown especially for their shape, like the acers or *Cornus controversa* 'Variegata', or potential magnificent soloists like the flowery *Cercis siliquastrum* (Judas tree), must be displayed in uncluttered space.

Container planting or bare root seasonal planting

When selecting plants from your local garden centre, you may choose to buy large specimens in containers to establish your garden quickly. These will cost more because they have been nurtured and repotted over a period of years, and they are often harder to establish in the ground than smaller plants, which adapt more quickly to their permanent site. Large specimens often suffer from shock when they are transplanted, and they will need staking and possibly even guy lines.

The advantages of buying plants in containers is that you may transplant them at more or less any time of year, as long as you avoid over-wet cold clay, frozen soil or a very hot, dry period. Buying bare-rooted plants requires forethought and patience. You will have to order them in advance so that they are delivered at the right planting time

A mature wine red Acer palmatum *Dissectum Atropurpureum Group blends well with azaleas.*

– usually in the autumn. Provided they are well packed from a reliable nursery, plants grown this way are usually successful starters, since they will have been grown in open ground and developed an efficient root system.

If a plant has been in the pot for too long and is 'pot bound', the congested roots will have spiralled round inside. These can prevent a transplanted plant from establishing a good root system in the ground and the plant may eventually die. When you are buying container-grown plants, look at the top of the compost. If it is compacted and encrusted with moss, lichen or even firmly established weeds, do not buy that plant.

In early summer the deep red foliage of Acer platanoides *'Crimson King' and the pink-tinged, cream leaves of* Acer pseudoplatanus *'Brilliantissimum' provide dramatic contrast against a green background.*

DESIGNING WITH TREES

When we are planning the look of the garden, four main attributes of trees influence our decisions.

Habit

All plants have a shape or form that is characteristic of their natural habit, and the profile of tree forms varies considerably. In large spaces, silhouettes of merging rounded forms provide a lush but undominating backcloth for the planned garden. Alternatively, individual specimens offer distinctive shapes that may be vertically narrow, widely spreading, rounded mounds or romantically weeping. These forms can determine the whole atmosphere of a garden. They can create formality by reinforcing geometric, vertical or horizontal lines, or they may suggest looser, flowing lines leading to more rhythmical, curved planting patterns.

There are narrow, upright fastigiate shapes, which are neatly tidy and almost sculptural in form, like the flowering cherry, *Prunus* 'Spire' (syn. *P.* 'Hillieri Spire'), *Sorbus × thuringiaca* 'Fastigiata', a hybrid between rowan and whitebeam, *Malus* 'Van Eseltine' and *Prunus* 'Amanogawa', all of which carry spring blossom. Many conifers come into this category. The dominant image of Italian gardens is that of the elegant Italian cypress, *Cupressus sempervirens* 'Stricta', repeated with geometric precision or grouped as a sculptured focus. For areas where the climate is too cold for the Italian cypress, less finely narrow conifers could be used, such as *Chamaecyparis lawsoniana* 'Columnaris Glauca' or *Taxus baccata* 'Fastigiata' – the former bluish, the latter almost black. All these eye-catching verticals add structure to the design of the garden, and this dominant shape may be echoed in the summer garden scene by groups of tall, upright perennials such as verbascums, delphiniums, crocosmias, phormiums, kniphofias and so forth.

This tiny dwarf Fagus sylvatica *'Purpurea Pendula' (weeping purple beech) contrasts with* Cornus alba *'Spaethii'. The tall grass* Miscanthus sacchariflorus *and the silvery perennial* Stachys byzantina *(syn.* S. lanata*) provide companion planting.*

It is accepted that formal garden styles use these vertical forms. But consider using them also as focal points in informal planting schemes, where, among the animation of summer, static aristocratic forms of this kind will create order, tempering the seasonal froth.

Weeping trees, on the other hand, are romantic in character and also work well in the informal garden. They create fluid curves of glissading linear patterns. The huge willow, *Salix × sepulcralis chrysocoma*, with a height and spread of 20m (75ft), needs a very large site to see it in all its beauty, and, of course, it associates happily with stretches of water. More manageable in scale is the weeping silver birch, *Betula pendula* 'Youngii', with a spread of 10m (30ft), or the weeping grey pear *Pyrus salicifolia* 'Pendula', which is even smaller, being 6m (20ft) by 5m (15ft). All float with the breeze and in summer suggest romantic plant associations of roses and honeysuckle.

Consider using similarly flowing summer perennials as visual associations with these trees: the softly curving leaves of the day lilies and agapanthus, or some of the grasses.

A few very small weeping trees have a more rigid, dense habit. *Fagus sylvatica* 'Purpurea Pendula' makes a 3m (10ft) mound of bronze-purple foliage. Some trees have a distinctly horizontal growth pattern, like *Cornus controversa* 'Variegata', a dogwood from Japan with a height and spread of nearly 15m (50ft). *Chimonanthus virginicus* (fringe tree) of North America also grows with a wide-spreading habit, more like that of a very large shrub. In maturity, the white Japanese cherry, *Prunus*

Famed for its horizontally tiered growth, Cornus controversa *'Variegata' graces all garden styles.*

'Shogetsu', may reach 5m (16ft) in height, but will stretch its branches nearly horizontally to create a flat crown some 8.5m (28ft) wide. And at a lower level, shrubs like *Viburnum plicatum* 'Mariesii' will flower in a succession of tiered horizontal planes.

Horizontals create a notion of tranquillity, and these rhythmical patterns in the summer scene can be levellers in more ways than one. Just as a sheet of water is beautiful among mounding willows, or the plane of a green expanse of grass is peaceful among flowerful perennials, so the effect of horizontal lines among the textures and colours of the summer garden creates unity. Flat-headed perennials, such as achilleas, scabious and anaphalis, or the sunward-facing daisies of *Echinacea purpurea* (cone flower) and rudbeckias, can be used to assist the linear rhythm.

Arching Sorbaria tomentosa var. angustifolia *(syn.* S. aitchisonii) *provides shade in which to sit. It will soon burst into panicles of white flowers.*

Such dominant forms set the scene when designing for summer. When the mind is on herbaceous glories, the character of the surrounding trees is not obvious. However, remove the backcloth, and the stage is more workshop than theatre.

Density

Equally important is the density of the canopy. Some trees allow light to filter through while others reduce the ground below to full shade. Beneath a silver birch like *Betula pendula* 'Tristis' or its counterpart the small yellow *B. p.* 'Golden Cloud', herbaceous plants can grow in lightly dappled shade. By contrast, the dense foliage of trees like the hawthorn, *Crataegus × lavallei,* or the densely leaved dark red maple, *Acer platanoides* 'Crimson King', prevents light from reaching the ground. Little light penetrates beneath the pretty but packed foliage of *Sorbaria tomentosa* var. *angustifolia* (syn. *S.aitchisonii*) as it arches 3m (10ft) overhead. Most gardens benefit in summer from restful shady places to provide cool relief on hot days, but in these areas of darkness, only selected plants like *Euphorbia amygdaloides* var. *robbiae, Iris foetidissima* or some of the ferns may grow.

Some trees are sparsely clad – some of the eucalyptus family, for example – others, like the widely spreading *Catalpa bignonioides* (Indian bean tree) or the tall, magnificent *Ailanthus altissima* (tree of heaven), have especially large leaves. It is important to consider the effect that each tree will have on the garden scene and how it may restrict or enhance planting possibilities.

Deciduous trees will have no canopy for several months each year, enabling spring bulbs and early herbaceous perennials to flower. But bear in mind that evergreen canopies will cut out the light throughout the year. Trees such as hollies and yew offer permanent shade, as do the much larger frost-hardy holm oak, *Quercus ilex*, and the kermes oak, *Q. coccifera*.

Summer blossom

It is, however, for their decorative potential that trees are often selected. Blossom is the great seducer, and three reliable genera of trees help us to launch the garden season and to provide late summer climax. In spring the Japanese cherries are the front runners, closely followed by the crab-apples *(Malus)*, and then the rowans *(Sorbus)*. To experience these trees heavy with flower is a reviving pleasure after winter. Some also offer late seasonal value in fruiting or autumn colour, thus extending colour in the garden well towards the end of the year.

Early in the year, magnolias display flowers of more sculpted style, and by late spring the hawthorns, lilacs, horse chestnuts and laburnums are in full flower. In early summer the tall, 15m (80ft), *Fraxinus ornus* (manna ash) produces foamy cream flowers, which are followed a few weeks later by those of the much smaller, 6m (20ft), slower growing *Fraxinus sieboldiana* (syn. *F. mariesii*). Both could link with other frothy flowers among the herbaceous plants, like aruncus and astilbes.

Trees with trailing racemes of flowers, like *Laburnum × watereri* 'Vossii', *Robinia × ambigua* 'Decaisneana' and *Robinia pseudoacacia* (false acacia) – all flowering in the earlier part of summer – could be associated with other trailing or arching flowers in the summer scene. In a sheltered but light situation, *Decaisnea fargesii* will trail finely delicate racemes of cream-green flowers, which in later summer become pendant blue fruits.

Sorbus cashmiriana *is a charming small tree, grown for its pink-edged, white flowers in spring, followed by clusters of white fruits at the end of the season.*

Among the more garden-sized summer-flowering trees there are some beauties. Lilacs may be bushes or small trees, and they launch the summer season with trusses of sweetly scented flowers. Really tiny trees are available, such as *Caragana arborescens* (pea tree) and grafted willows and euonymus. Wider but not tall are forms of the *Cornus* genus, carrying bracts that look like flowers. *Tamarix ramosissima* (syn. *T. pentandra*) 'Rubra' (the tamarisk) may be grown as a small tree, reaching, at most, 3m (9ft). *Buddleja alternifolia* is also really a shrub, often grown on a single stem, with trails of fragrant lilac-coloured flowers.

Trailing racemes of flowers are a virtue of the robinias. *Robinia* × *ambigua* 'Decaisneana', 10m (33ft), has pink flower trails in midsummer similar to those of *R.* × *slavinii* 'Hillieri', which is manageably smaller. The mop-head acacia, *R. pseudoacacia* 'Inermis', is a neat lollipop, and *R. p.* 'Rozynskiana' is elegantly put together. Erect panicles of yellow flowers in mid- to late summer are provided by the broad-headed *Koelreuteria paniculata* (golden rain tree) from India, which reaches 5m (16ft). Larger trees are the attractively named *Albizia julibrissin* (silk tree) and *Cercis siliquastrum* (Judas tree), which flower in high summer, but both need protection, as does *Myrtus communis* ssp. *tarentina* (aromatic myrtle).

Foliage

Pretty foliage can be as valued as flowers. *Robinia pseudoacacia* 'Frisia' is a summery yellow and is in constant demand. *Gleditsia triacanthos* 'Sunburst' is also yellow but a slower grower, and I prefer the dark claret leaves of *G. t.* 'Rubylace'. Acers are the other most decoratively foliaged trees to play a part throughout summer, and there are variegated forms as well as plain colours. These may contrast with or complement the summer flower scheme.

Malus floribunda, *heavy with flowers, announces the start of summer.*

23

3 · SHRUBS FOR STRUCTURE

The value of shrubs is thought to be largely a spring issue, and many of them certainly give their flowering best early in the year. Nevertheless, as one of the mainstays of the whole garden, shrubs are indispensable and play a significant role in the whole scene. Evergreens create all-year structure, and deciduous plants provide foliage patterns, textures and colours for six months or more.

Shrubs, like trees, provide the 'bones' of garden design. They, too, may be tall and thin, like the acid-loving *Embothrium coccineum* Lanceolatum Group (Chilean fire bush), or squat and bulging, like *Hebe cupressoides* 'Boughton Dome'. Or they may be anonymous for eleven months of the year and gloriously notable for one, like *Forsythia* 'Beatrix Farrand'. They may have a distinct sculptural

Topiaried box and tailing variegated ivy provide year-round greenery in a passage-way that never sees the sun.

24

presence like *Mahonia lomariifolia* or be formlessly flattering to others, a role often played by *Prunus lusitanica* (Portuguese laurel). Some are richly textured with tiny leaves, like *Cotoneaster horizontalis* and *Lonicera pileata*, while others carry large, beautiful leaves, as with the Chinese *Hydrangea aspera* ssp. *sargentiana,* which is noted for its huge velvety foliage.

When you are placing shrubs in your garden plan it is important to consider their ultimate sizes and relate them to the herbaceous plants in the garden. Their massed forms may act as a boundary or they could be integrated into a mixed planting scheme. They add height and may even provide the apex of a triangular grouping.

All of these assets can be worked into your summer scheme. Always bear in mind that gardens are never static and that plants grow and alter, so no arrangement can ever be permanent. The closest one can come to permanence is by using evergreen shrubs.

EVERGREENS

Truly valuable for creating structure in the garden plan are the evergreens. Many of these are so modest that their existence is barely noticeable in summer, but how they would be missed in winter. They are as important as masonry, fulfilling the same functions as space-dividing walls, room enclosures, boundary markers, picture frames and sculptural foci.

Shape and form

Some evergreens, like yew, box, *Ligustrum ovalifolium* (privet), escallonia and varieties of lonicera, may be rigidly clipped into hedges or even topiary. But many evergreen shrubs are valuable because they grow with a naturally structured form and may be used as 'spot' plants to draw the eye. Plants such as *Phormium tenax* (New Zealand flax) and

Yucca gloriosa, for example, have dominant, spiked foliage. Sculptural shapes may be used to emphasize changes in garden character, acting as markers where formal style ends and informal style begins. Many different shapes can be used for this, from clipped obelisks of yew to rounded hebes like *Hebe cupressoides* 'Boughton Dome'.

Flowering evergreen shrubs

Evergreens with flowers as well are a blessing. Some of the viburnums, like *V.* × *burkwoodii*, which is 1.8m (6ft), and *V. davidii*, are very appropriate, and the escallonias like *E.* 'Donard Star' provide rose-pink flowers up to 1.5m (5ft) although they may lose their leaves in cold exposed conditions. *Choisya ternata*, with its glossy bright

Philadelphus 'Virginal' spreads its fragrance around the garden in early summer.

25

green leaves, grows to about 2.5m (8ft) and has wonderfully scented white flowers in early to midsummer. Sometimes there is a second flowering in late summer. Evergreen varieties of berberis are also floriferous – *B. gagnepainii* var. *lanceifolia* is 1.5m (5ft) tall and laden with yellow flowers in early summer.

Background cover

Evergreen can also mean 'eversilver' or 'evergold', both of which offer useful permanent colour to the outdoor scene. Santolinas, lavenders and small euonymus will provide reliable foliage back-up during 'dead' periods throughout summer.

Some gentle evergreen foliage effects occur with the New Zealanders *Pittosporum* 'Garnettii', which reaches over 3m (10ft) and has greyish variegated white with pink leaves, or *P. tenuifolium* 'Irene Paterson', which has marbled leaves. The deep red *P. t.* 'Purpureum' is tender but adds blackened ruby-purple colour, while *P. t.* 'Warnham Gold' has sun yellow foliage and, unlike the others, undulate leaves, which allow these attractive shrubs to merge well with the colours of summer flowers. Choose white, pink, red and powder blue flowers with the first three and creamy yellows, rusty oranges and deep blues with the latter.

Some evergreens, like *Viburnum rhytidophyllum,* a tall shrub of 3m (10ft), and *Prunus laurocerasus* (laurel), of about the same height, provide contrast with their rich foliage.

Viburnum rhytido-phyllum is a tall evergreen shrub noted for its bold, coarsely textured leaves. Here it is shown in full flower.

One of the prettiest evergreens, the marbled Pittosporum tenuifolium *'Irene Paterson' needs protection in cold winters.*

Conifers

In discussing evergreens one cannot ignore conifers, which offer such a variety of shapes and colour. Here, eventual size and speed of growth must be considered. Even 'dwarf' conifers aim high, many reaching heights and spreads of over 1.5m (5ft).

Taxus baccata (yew) has been used for centuries as a backing shrub. Yews are strong, long-lived and provide a dense background, though a few are golden, like the evergold English yew *T. b.* 'Semperaurea'. All are hardy, but the hardiest, the Japanese yew, *T. cuspidata,* will withstand very low temperatures. All the yews work well with mixed planting.

Some yews are useful hedging plants. Others, like *T. b.* 'Fastigiata', which has a narrow, upright habit, and *T. b.* 'Dovastoniana' (the Westfelton yew), which grows in wide, horizontal tiers, have impressive and distinctive forms.

During summer, many herbaceous plants are flattered when planted in association with junipers or false cypress (*Chamaecyparis*). Do also consider planting columns of *Juniperus communis* 'Hibernica' (the Irish juniper) or the pencil-slim *Juniperus scopulorum* 'Skyrocket' as accent plants to make formal shapes among mixed planting.

At a lower level rounded shapes also have their uses in providing a static simplicity. *Chamaecyparis lawsoniana* 'Gimbornii' or *C. obtusa* 'Nana', both richly

Evergreen Abies procera *'Glauca Prostrata' provides a silver-blue background for the cluster of neat dwarf* Juniperus communis *'Compressa'. The group is carpeted by* Acaena *'Blue Haze', which is also evergreen.*

White Lychnis coronaria *Oculata Group and* Veronicastrum virginicum *f.* album *(syn.* Veronica virginica *f.* alba*) are superbly displayed because of the deep plum-brown of a copper beech hedge behind.*

green, provide rock-like stability to any good planting scheme, while many of the small conifers work extremely well with the low sub-shrubs of summer.

DECORATIVE DECIDUOUS SHRUBS

A framework of deciduous shrubs chosen for their ornamental qualities can create a strong setting for summer perennials. Soil requirements and site conditions need to be assessed first, however. Calcifuges – rhododendrons and pieris, for example – will need acid soils; cistus prefer sun and sandy soil to dank clay; escallonias will readily withstand salt sea breezes, but will not do well in

cold inland sites or in temperatures below freezing. Your environment will affect your selection.

Once you are confident that your selected shrubs will like their home, you will need to give thought to how they will relate to other plants in the summer garden. You will have chosen your evergreens first; now you must think about your intended colour scheme.

Colour in foliage

Shrubs can be chosen either to contrast with or to echo the virtues of herbaceous perennials, and either way the effects can be very satisfying.

You could use the dark plain colours of *Corylus maxima* 'Purpurea' to set off the silvery foliage and feathery flowers of gypsophila. Or you could choose a more tranquil effect by picking shrubs that work more subtly with their fellows in the herbaceous border. For example, in sunlight the silver foliage of artemisia may be egged on by a thoughtfully sited *Elaeagnus angustifolia* with its similar silvered effect.

Japanese acers

Varieties of *Acer palmatum* (Japanese palmate maples) deserve a section to themselves. These queens of the garden merit special attention and can grace any garden with their elegance. They can be grown as specimens but also companionably in some mixed schemes. On the whole they are slow-growing, but will eventually develop into small, airy trees. It is well worth becoming familiar with the many subtleties of leaf shape and colour. *Acer palmatum* 'Osakazuki' has a mid-green, neatly delineated seven-lobed leaf, which gives no hint of the extraordinary glowing red in the autumn, any more than the larger foliage of *A. japonicum* 'Viti-folium' indicates its glorious autumn rage. *A. palmatum* 'Linearilobum' is very finely cut and floats in the breeze.

For pure butter yellow through the season the slow-growing *A. p.* 'Aureum' is unbeatable. But red-leaved maples are probably the most popular. *A. p.* 'Bloodgood' is a particularly fine purple-red form. The leaves progress from being slightly bronze at the very start of the season to rich maroon most of the summer.

I cannot leave the maples without referring to *A. p.* 'Senkaki' (coral bark maple), an elegantly green-leaved form, which graduates to canary yellow in autumn. The stems are a vividly attractive coral colour in winter.

Flowering shrubs

The flowering shrubs should be chosen for the harmony of their relationship with the flowers of summer herbaceous plants. The colours may be chosen to work within the scheme or they may add white as a calming balance. To make selection easier, I have divided these into three main periods of summer flowering.

Early summer There are some distinguished names to be recorded here but once flowering is over, these shrubs tend to be rather anonymous, even ungainly, so site them where herbaceous plants can take over. Early summer brings the

All the cultivars of Acer palmatum *are attractive, and, as can be seen, this specimen of the Dissectum Viride Group is characteristically finely elegant. Here it hangs above a pool with* Caltha palustris var. radicans *'Flore Pleno' as a marginal plant.*

The beauty bush, Kolkwitzia amabilis *'Pink Cloud', flowers in early summer.*

blossom, this beautiful plant is only 1.5m (5ft) tall but is wide spreading and requires at least 2.4m (8ft).

The beauty bush, *Kolkwitzia amabilis* 'Pink Cloud', is ravishingly pretty when its elegant, 3m (10ft) high arching form is covered with small pink bells, and, if your garden beds contain acid soil, do consider planting cultivars of *Kalmia latifolia* (calico bush), which are of a similar height and covered in pink-red flower clusters. There is no better sight in early summer.

High summer By midsummer fuchsias, abutilons, escallonias, potentillas and cistus present a colour range from purple through to pinks, yellows and oranges. In full sun, potentillas may flower for four months.

Requiring restraint, but floriferous in the extreme, buddleias begin to flaunt in early summer, and some continue through until autumn. The tall hardy buddleias must be cut back hard in early spring to prevent them from growing into top-heavy trees. A smaller variety, *Buddleja davidii* 'Nanho Blue', is suitable for smaller gardens.

Lower shrubs, such as potentillas, hebes, lavenders, sages, halimiocistus and hypericums, are also manageably small.

Correctly pruned, the Californian lilac (*Ceanothus*) is a genus that provides cultivars for all of the summer months. Some are deciduous, some are evergreen, some are frost hardy. All can be heavy with blue flowers, pale or intense. They are worth taking trouble over because pure blue flowers on large shrubs are not very common in midsummer.

Late summer Many of the late summer shrubs do, however, have blue flowers. *Perovskia atriplicifolia* and *Caryopteris* × *clandonensis* are rather undisciplined low shrubs with a wide-spreading habit. Both should be severely pruned in spring, and both carry blue flowers with a hint of lavender in the hue. They can be very charming with their silver-grey foliage. Another late summer blue is the vivid *Ceratostigma willmottianum,* a Chinese dwarf

fragrant benefits of the smaller lilacs like *Syringa microphylla* 'Superba', which are not particularly beautiful at other times of year but whose flowering and pervasive perfume have seduced many people into growing them. There is a lot of white blossom in early summer, and both philadelphus and deutzias play a major role. The philadelphus are among the most fragrant plants in the garden; some are double flowered and some single. *Exochorda* × *macrantha* 'The Bride' must be included, too. Generously covered in lush white

shrub with rich mid-blue flowers. It is 80cm (2ft 6in) tall and should be cut back in spring. All blend well with the colours of late summer. Both lavateras and hydrangeas mark the final summer fling, adding pink and white to blues.

Floral hedging

Some fuchsias make successful informal hedging. *F.* 'Riccartonii', with small red and purple flowers, is probably the best and will reach 1.5m (5ft).

The hibiscus, too, can be used to make a good informal barrier. Being larger flowered, they merge well with herbaceous perennials as well as with their more shrubby peers. Blue, mauve and crimson set the cool tones of their flower colours. Given a sunny site with rich soil and careful pruning in spring, by late summer they are covered with large mallow-like flowers.

The evergreen escallonia can be clipped to form a tight hedge, and is in great demand in areas beside the sea. The flowering period may extend to early autumn and the red, white or apple-blossom flowers will survive early clipping.

Some of the lower hedging shrubs may be tightly clipped but will expand with flower in summer. Lavenders like the dwarf *Lavandula angustifolia* 'Hidcote' and *L. a.* 'Twickel Purple'

Buddleja davidii *in full flower dominates a mixed planting bed in summer.*

make marvellous scented restraints for a rose or herb bed. All need pruning early in the year or they become leggy monsters. *L. stoechas* (French lavender) needs a gentler climate with very little frost, but is notable for its pretty form, and *L. viridis* from southwest Europe is another less hardy but unusual white-flowered lavender with lemon-scented foliage.

Santolinas may also be used for low hedges. They range from the grey-leaved *Santolina chamaecyparissus* (cotton lavender) to the almost silvery *S. pinnata*, but the flowers tend to be a rather harsh yellow ochre, and they may need to be removed.

Scents

Many shrubs contribute more than their looks to the sense of summer. They may provide heavy aromatic fragrances or light sweet perfumes; some have the distinct smell of fruits. *Cytisus battandieri*, a tall broom from Morocco, with spikes of pure yellow flowers against silky silver leaves, has a scent reminiscent of pineapples.

A far heavier scent comes from another yellow-flowered shrub, *Jasminum humile* 'Revolutum', and *Ptelea trifoliata* 'Aurea' (more of a tree than a shrub) has golden leaves and green flowers with a delicious fragrance.

All these shrubs flower in midsummer and would look attractive surrounded by the steely blue of *Eryngium × oliverianum,* a pale blue haze of flax, *Linum narbonense* or massed *Anaphalis triplinervis*, with its grey leaves and white flowers.

For a richer fragrance, the flowers of the myrtle, particularly of *Myrtus communis* ssp. *tarentina*, are delicious. The shrub is best grown on a warm wall where the fragrance will be pervasive.

Towards the end of high summer, with both Hydrangea paniculata *'Floribunda' and* H. macrophylla *'Mariesii Perfecta' (syn. H. m. 'Blue Wave') in full flower, gold day lilies and deep blue agapanthus integrate superbly.*

DESIGNING WITH SHRUBS

Ceanothus *'Puget Blue'* has a height and spread of up to 1.2m (4ft). A dense evergreen, it bears rich blue flowers in spring. Grow it in a sunny site, protected from wind and frost.

In this border design, shrubs provide the framework for herbaceous plants. This is the most easily maintained part of the garden.

The border is 2.7m (9ft) deep by 11m (36ft) long. Some of the plants, like the cotoneaster, are 3m (10ft) tall and will overhang the group. Others, like the ceanothus, vitis, escallonia and chaenomeles, are best grown on a wall.

When planning this garden, the choice of shrubs is based, first, on their ultimate size and then on the shapes they create.

Evergreens such as elaeagnus, viburnum, ceanothus, escallonia, hebe, halimiocistus, lavender, santolina and cistus provide a framework all year round. The phormium provides vertical shape, and the hebe, cistus and *Viburnum davidii* provide rounded profiles.

Long-lasting foliage colour influenced the selection. Gold-splashed elaeagnus, red cotinus, berberis and phormium, plus silver-grey lavender and santolina last for months. In the autumn, rich scarlets contrast with yellow-berried cotoneaster, purple-fruited callicarpa and blue-berried viburnum.

To provide flowers through the season, there is the sequential flowering of chaenomeles, cistus, potentilla, lavender, halimiocistus, hebe and clematis. In autumn, the ceratostigma is vivid blue followed by the violet-coloured fruits of the callicarpa.

Soil preparation begins in the previous autumn by turning over the whole shrub bed to a depth of approximately 60cm (2ft). Loosen the subsoil with a fork, but do not bring it to the surface. Mix in well-rotted manure with a topsoil fertilizer such as bonemeal or super-phosphate.

Plant bare-rooted shrubs from then through to spring unless your local conditions are too extreme. Always avoid frost and water-logged conditions when planting. The planting hole must be wide enough to spread the roots – that is 60–90cm (2–3ft). The depth is usually 35-45cm

In high summer this town garden is luxuriously foliaged and awash with flowers. Shrub roses, cistus, lavender and lavatera are some of the shrubs among which geraniums, achillea, poppies and alchemilla mix well.

(15–18in). Do not plant deeper than the soil ring on the plant, which indicates its original planting depth. Water thoroughly and mulch. Firm in and check this again after winter, when frost or the wind may have loosened the plant.

Containerized shrubs may be planted at other times of year. Soak the shrub in the container for at least an hour before transplanting.

Gently loosen the plant from the pot with minimal root disturbance. If the roots are coiled, tease them out before planting. Fill the immediate surround of the plant ball with a fine soil and peat mix. Water, then add a surface mulch.

Key to plants
1. *Elaeagnus × ebbingei* 'Limelight'
2. *Viburnum davidii* (one male, one female)
3. *Cotoneaster salicifolius* 'Exburyensis'
4. *Ceratostigma willmottianum*
5. *Santolina chamaecyparissus* 'Lemon Queen' (cotton lavender)
6. *Phormium tenax* Purpureum Group
7. *Salvia officinalis* 'Icterina' (golden sage)
8. *Cistus × hybridus* (syn. *C. × corbariensis*)
9. *Ceanothus* 'Puget Blue'
10. *Vitis vinifera* 'Purpurea'
11. *Escallonia* 'Donard Radiance'
12. *Potentilla fructicosa* 'Abbotswood'
13. *Berberis thunbergii* 'Bagatelle'
14. *Lavandula stoechas*
15. *Callicarpa bodinieri*
16. *Cotinus* 'Grace'
17. *Hebe* 'Midsummer Beauty'
18. *Salvia officinalis* Purpurascens Group
19. *Halimiocistus sahucii*
20. *Viburnum plicatum* 'Watanabe'
21. *Chaenomeles speciosa* 'Nivalis'
22. *Deutzia crenata* var. *nakaiana* 'Nikko'
23. *Hebe albicans* 'Red Edge'
24. *Clematis* 'Polish Spirit'

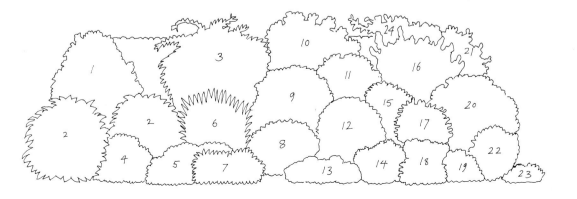

4 · ROSES TO REDISCOVER

Viola cornuta and lavender are wonderful companions for roses. This is the Musk rose R. 'Cornelia'.

Valued by the Egyptians, the Persians and in ancient Rome, the rose has been popular in most cultures throughout the centuries. Truly a case of 'age cannot wither her nor custom stale her infinite variety', the rose has graced the large garden and the small, the famous and the modest, those in the East and the West.

Roses may be delicate and small, covering a shrub with the fragile effect of butterflies, or they may be heavily petalled, lush and exotic. The colours range from dense black-velvet red to fluorescent pinks, pure ivory, apricot and deep yellows. The yellow roses largely originated with the Persian rose, which extended the colour range to

include oranges and even browns. Serious attempts at creating a blue rose are close to success, although I must admit to being unmoved. Scent has long been part of the appeal, from heavy musk to a light summer sweetness. Some roses carry aromatic leaves. The fragrance of a rose garden in summer is one of its greatest pleasures.

Foliage, too, provides attractive alternatives, and some is nearly evergreen. There are simple glossy shapes, finely cut smaller leaves and a few are coloured shades of grey. The foliage of some roses contributes to the glories of autumn, while hips may be black, yellow, orange, scarlet or crimson. Some develop in small clusters; others are fat and full; others have bottle shapes. These roses are sought after when planning a border for the end of the season.

DESIGN

Roses may be compact and neat or huge and rambling. You may decide to design a formal rose garden on strict geometric principles, as shown on the plan at the end of this chapter, or you may decide to grow them in an informal manner, allowing them to mingle with each other in romantically curved beds. Shrub roses merge well in a mixed shrub and herbaceous scheme, whereas the formal Large Flowered (Hybrid Tea) roses are far better grown alone. To know how to design with roses it is important to understand the great differences of habit and character, so in this chapter I have separated the types and suggested ways of growing them.

Large Flowered roses (Hybrid Teas)

During the early years of this century flower perfection became the driving aim of rose breeders. This led to the often disease-resistant, reliable Hybrid Tea roses, popular with both private and public gardeners. Now renamed 'Large Flowered', these roses have dominated the gardens of the twentieth century – until recently.

Today, the emphasis has moved away from these specimen roses as they do not mix easily with other plants. The whole garden scene is now important, and an isolated bed of the Large Flowered rose has become rather outdated. Magnificent though the blooms may be, they do not cooperate with other plants; indeed, they relate none too well with each other. Sometimes this problem has been overcome by limiting the colour selection – for example, planning red-pink beds and orange-yellow beds. The strongly coloured image is powerful from a distance and magnificent close up, yet it lacks charm, and the result is strangely unaffecting.

Rosa 'Graham Thomas' is a new Large Flowered rose. It is wonderfully fragrant and is a rich golden-yellow. It has an elegant habit and is very vigorous.

The intense red of Rosa *'Scarlet Fire' is eye-catching among other plants such as* Cistus ladanifer.

Old Shrub roses

Many Old Shrub roses would have been familiar to gardeners of the last century, who used them in the cottage garden, and some were familiar long ago to gardening monks working in medieval monastery gardens, where medicinal and culinary needs dominated enclosed spaces.

The Old Shrub roses vary greatly in both habit and type of flower. Unlike other shrubs, which tend to have only one brief major flower flush, often in early summer, some of the older Shrub roses will flower for weeks or have two flowering periods, at the start and the end of summer.

Species roses The origins of the roses that we know today are the species, the wild roses from around the world. Some of these are still valued in gardens. Many are very tall and benefit from the support of a wall, but most are free-standing, tall bushes of 2.1m (7ft) or more, possessing an elegant, arching habit that can lighten the more 'solid' forms of some shrubs, such as viburnums, mahonias, berberis, choisya, cotoneasters and the laurels. The untamed look of the species rose is equally at home with rural plants like elder and dogwoods. The fine habit is often enhanced with 'ferny' foliage, which in some cases is softly pewter-grey, like that of *Rosa rubrifolia,* or the feathery leaves of the threepenny-bit rose *R. farreri* var. *persetosa,* which become crimson in autumn.

The flowers of *Rosa* species are usually delicately single, and although they appear once only, are often followed by a mass of hips. I have an affection for *R. xanthina* f. *hugonis,* which flowers at the very beginning of summer to a height of about 2m (6ft) and carries pale yellow single flowers among its fern-like leaves. Another lovely early yellow is *R. primula* (incense rose), which has aromatic foliage. Both look charming with scillas, myosotis, vinca, campanulas and nigella, and in late summer caryopteris could add successive blue tones at the base.

So how can we make these Large Flowered roses work in the total summer garden scene? Try grouping them together in separate and one-colour units to form a detail of the garden picture as a whole. For example, a mass of the copper-red 'Just Joey', fringe-ringed with *Alchemilla mollis* (lady's mantle) or *Iris germanica* would be a success. They would also be seen at their best within formal beds, outlined with clipped box. Plant all-white roses, such as 'Pascali', with blue forget-me-nots, succeeded by *Nepeta racemosa* (syn. *N. mussinii*; catmint), or the yellow 'Graham Thomas' with *Sisyrinchium striatum* or blue geraniums.

For hips, consider *R.* 'Cantabrigiensis', *R. moyesii* varieties, *R. forrestiana, R.* 'Doncasteri' and *R. villosa* (syn. *R. pomifera)*. All are heavy with flaming red and orange fruit in late summer, some in dense clusters and others with elongated flask-like form. The very pretty small burnet rose, *R. pimpinellifolia* (syn. *R. spinosissima),* is also worth heeding, as its massed white flowers are followed by black hips. It is ideal for the smaller garden.

Some species roses have other assets. Many, such as *R. setipoda, R. multibracteata* and *R. eglanteria*, the sweet briar, have aromatic foliage. *R. rubrifolia* has grey-purple leaves against reddish stems, and in a silver border with artemisias, lavenders, white-flowering *Anthemis punctata* ssp. *cupaniana,* all overlooked by *Pyrus salicifolia* 'Pendula' (weeping pear), it never fails to appeal.

One species rose, *R. sericea* ssp *omeiensis* f. *pteracantha* (syn. *R. omeiensis* f. *pteracantha),* is grown not only for its pretty ferny foliage but also for its strikingly unusual thorns, which, flattened, lengthy and translucently ruby-coloured, glint in the sunshine as if they were red amber. It will make burglar-proof hedging, prettied up by ferny foliage, as will the tough, thorny *R. fedtschenkoana,* which has pale green-grey foliage, single white flowers and a transgressing suckering habit.

The species roses link well with flowering shrubs like philadelphus, syringa, escallonia and hebes; less satisfactorily, I feel, with calcifuges such as rhododendrons, pieris and camellias. The rather fussily leaved potentillas, which offer a similar flower shape, do nothing for species roses, whereas more dominantly foliaged varieties of *Cistus* do. Many of these roses also look very fetching with the clearly defined large leaves of the tree peonies, which provide charm in the garden long after their flowers have finished.

Contrasting foliage, like the narrow reedy leaves of iris, libertia, hemerocallis and sisyrinchium, always looks well with roses. Gentler forms of flowering perennials like *Alchemilla mollis* (lady's

mantle), geraniums, catmint, campanulas, some heucheras and achilleas can be alluring at their base.

Rugosa roses These merit consideration. Never elegant, but tough, generously hipped and densely foliaged, these wild roses with their large flowers in different colours come from China and Japan and are quite distinctive. They make excellent hedges, and are substantial enough to hold their own against softer foliage like that of the acers. Like the species roses, they are well suited to an informal setting, where they mingle easily with *Cornus* varieties, *Viburnum opulus, Sambucus racemosa* and other 'wilder' planting schemes.

The scented and reliable Hybrid Musk Rosa *'Penelope' flowers continuously, producing creamy, salmon pink, semi-double flowers. It grows to 1.5m (5ft) high with a spread of 2m (6ft).*

Other Old Shrub roses Among other 'old-fashioned' Shrub roses, even the names have enormous appeal: Musk, Damask, Bourbon, Moss and Gallica are all rather evocative words, confirming the romance of the rose. For the glories of summer and for almost continuous flowering, the Portland Damasks, Bourbons, Chinas and Hybrid Perpetuals are remarkable. Some of them are very large, but others are more manageable – it is wise to check. Most fall into the cool pinks, crimson, maroon or white range of colour, so associating flowers should be in the blue-based colour ranges.

Some of the Hybrid Perpetuals are invaluable for adding intense deep purple-reds to the summer scene. R. 'Empereur du Maroc' has intensely dark velvet richness of colour, and the deeply maroon, luxuriantly petalled flowers are very fragrant. I prefer R. 'Souvenir du Docteur Jamain', which is slightly taller, slightly redder and has quite outstanding perfume.

R. 'Ferdinand Pichard', a Bourbon, has maroon and white striped petals. Of the striped roses, this is the one with the greatest clarity in the pattern; it is also reliable, well foliaged and richly scented.

The repeat-flowering Portland Damask, R. 'Madame Knorr' (syn. 'Comte de Chambord'), is suitable for smaller gardens. It is a vigorous pink rose, very full, with quartered petal pattern, and also lightly scented. Another lower growing favourite of mine, R. × odorata 'Pallida (syn. 'Old Blush China'), has clusters of pale lilac-pink blooms, which sometimes continue to flower right through the autumn. It is thought to have been known in China over 1,000 years ago.

Among the oldest and most revered of the Shrub roses, the Gallicas provide magnificent, richly scented but smaller plants, though the same blue-based colours of crimson, maroon, purple

Surrounded by blue nepeta, the Old Shrub rose R. gallica *var.* officinalis *(apothecary's rose) is a deep red, and* R. gallica *'Versicolor' (syn.* R. mundi*) is delicately striped. In the distance a pink peony echoes the colour.*

41

The flowers of Rosa gallica *'Versicolor' (syn.* R. mundi*) are splashed pink and white on a crimson ground. This rose is believed to have been known in the twelfth century.*

Opposite: *Silver-foliaged artemisias,* A. ludoviciana *'Silver Queen' and* A. l. *'Valerie Finnis', provide a wonderful accompaniment for the pink Shrub rose* R. *'Aloha'.*

and lilac-pink are characteristic. *R.* 'Belle de Crécy' is outstanding, cerise-pink flowers fading to lavender-mauve. *R. gallica* 'Versicolor' (*R. mundi*) is another striped rose, probably the oldest. Its former name, *Rosa mundi*, referred to 'Fair Rosamund', mistress of Henry II of England in the twelfth century. For intense magenta purple, *R.* 'Tuscany Superb' and *R.* 'Charles de Mills' are desirable. The low-growing Gallica *R.* × *franco-furtana* (syn. 'Empress Josephine') is a rose of quality, with large intense pink flowers with ruffled petals followed by hips. It was a favourite of the Empress, who gave it its former name.

There are also many wonderful, softly coloured roses among the summer flowering Albas, Centifolias and Damasks. The shell pink of the Centifolia *R.* 'Fantin-Latour' is subtly different from the blush pink *R.* 'Great Maiden's Blush', an old Alba rose, admired for over five hundred years. The magnificent Alba 'Königin von Dänemark' grows to 1.5m (5ft). Its fragrance is sweetly strong, and the pink is at first relatively dark until the blooms open to a quartered rose. *R.* × *damascena semperflorens* (syn. *R.* × *d. bifera*, sometimes known as 'Autumn Damask' or 'Quatre Saisons', is 1.5m (5ft) and has a looser ruffled arrangement of pink petals. It too is highly scented. Another Damask, *R.* 'Madame Hardy', is pure white, developing from a simple cup form to a flattened flower and reaching 1.8m (6ft). Siting these old summer roses in the garden is a pleasure. They group well together, and smaller ones may be massed in threes

The Shrub rose R. 'Tuscany' is a claret red. The Modern Shrub rose R. 'William Shakespeare' echoes the colour, which is further reinforced by the intense maroon reds of Lychnis coronaria *and* Geranium psilostemon *(syn. G. armenum).*

or fives. By using them together, the long flowering period of some will support the more limited midsummer display of others.

Because the colour range is so restricted, in that all the red-pinks are blue based, blue flowers such as delphiniums, scabious, salvias, anchusas, agapanthus and campanulas will all blend in beautifully. Tall delphiniums will need as much space to themselves as the roses, but plants like *Viola cornuta* and *Campanula persicifolia* 'Telham Beauty' may gently work their way among the roses. Pink flowers can also be used, but they should always be the cooler tones. *Geranium* × *oxonianum* 'Wargrave Pink' is reliable and long flowering, and *G. pratense* 'Plenum Violaceum', with violet overtones, makes a magnificent companion.

For ground-covering awkward spaces between the shrub roses *G. macrorrhizum* is a splendid weed suppressor, with small pink flowers and aromatic foliage. Dicentras, artemisias and dianthus associate sympathetically with roses. So does the white *Phlox maculata* 'Omega'. *Geranium renardii* and *G. clarkei* 'Kashmir White', frothy *Gypsophila paniculata* 'Bristol Fairy', white *Thalictrum aquilegiifolium,* white agapanthus and grey-leaved *Anaphalis margaritacea* will all add vivacity

The deep claret red roses can be echoed with some attractive perennials – *Knautia macedonica* (syn. *Scabiosa rumelica*) or *Cirsium rivulare* var. *atropurpureum,* for example. *Geranium psilostemon* (syn. *G. armenum*) will create pin-point spots of maroon and magenta among the border plants, while *G. phaeum* 'Mourning Widow' adds small black-maroon nodding flowers.

When it comes to selecting structural plants to go with the roses, clipped yew, *Taxus baccata,* cannot be beaten as an enclosing hedge, and *Buxus sempervirens* (box) always associates well, framing the planting space. Alternatively, the silver-greys of lavender, santolina and teucrium can be used to make softly retaining hedging.

Modern Shrub roses A most useful group of Shrub roses are those developed more recently, by hybridizing species roses with old roses. They have all the quality and style of the past, but are usually sturdier and more disease resistant. These Modern Shrub roses have many good characteristics of the old roses, often bearing trusses of fragrant, multi-petalled, Centifolia-like roses. *R.* 'William Shakespeare', one of the new rose breeds, has the wonderful purple-crimson and the scent of the old roses, but rather more shapely flowers, and it grows to a manageable 1m (3ft 3in).

Patio roses Bearing in mind that many of us now have restricted plots, cluster-flowered shrub roses, which grow to about 1m (3ft 3in), have fulfilled a need. *R.* 'The Fairy', with its small pale pink blooms, is in flower for months. *R.* 'Ballerina' is similar but with darker pink flowers. Recently, smaller 'Patio' roses, which are cluster-flowered, perpetual and reliable, have become available. These are ideal for town gardens and associate well with paving. Among them are what are known as the 'County Series' in Britain. These include *R.* 'Kent' (syn. 'Poulcov'), a compact pure white, *R.* 'Norfolk' (syn. 'Poulfolk'), a cheerful fragrant yellow, *R.* 'Rutland' (syn. 'Poulshine'), a lovely soft pink and *R.* 'Suffolk' (syn. 'Kormixal'), a brilliant scarlet. Experiment with a few of these types to create the effect you desire in the rose garden.

There are many other modern roses that are beautifully formed shrubs. The hybridizers are now considering all the qualities of the rose – its habit, foliage, disease resistance, scent and hips – and there will be more beauties to come. Those mentioned are but a few, and I recommend the reader to pursue the subject. For summer, there can be no finer flower than the rose.

Above: Rosa 'Buff Beauty', a Hybrid Musk, is a vigorous and very beautiful rose, carrying trusses of yellow-apricot flowers, which become parchment-coloured as they fade. Its fragrant flowers appear in midsummer and continue until the end of the season. It grows to 2m (6ft) tall with the same spread.

Left: Rosa 'The Fairy' is a small polyantha-flowered, Patio rose, with a maximum height and spread of 1m (3ft 3in). It flowers throughout the season but must be dead-headed.

DESIGN FOR A ROSE GARDEN

This rose garden is enclosed by yew hedging on three sides but the fourth side has an open view allowing sunlight through trellis. The design is traditional and the roses create the romantic character of the garden. It will be at its best for three to four months in summer. The garden is 14 × 16m (46 × 52ft). Two rose tunnels lead to a central pool of water, which is surrounded by white irises.

Most of the roses shown are Old and Modern Shrub roses. When roses are selected the ultimate size must be considered, because even when pruned hard, they will always grow back to their natural height before reaching their full flowering potential.

Plant rose shrubs bare-rooted in the autumn if possible. Soak the roots for at least an hour and plant in a hole big enough for the spread-out roots. Fill in with damp compost or well-rotted manure,

Opposite: Rosa 'Ballerina', seen grown as a standard, looks wonderful in formal rose gardens among clipped box hedging.

good soil and bone meal. Roses prefer slightly acidic soil, but are adaptable. They also require well-drained but moisture-retaining conditions.

Roses grown in containers may be planted throughout the year if the soil is not frozen or flooded. Always soak the plant in the container before gently removing and planting it. If the roots curl round, tease them out before planting. Prune to about 15cm (6in) from the ground in the first season, mulch and water thoroughly and mulch again. Firm in and check regularly during the first year for signs of wind rock.

Perennials can be used to cover the bare foot of the 'leggy' rose bushes and provide flower colours of powder blue, cream, white and dark red. These may be planted at the same time or in late spring. Foliage plants add evergreen silvers and greens as well as textures. Dark yew hedging is a flattering background for every plant in the plan. Supplementing the rose climbers are varieties of clematis.

Fine gravel paths and small granite setts provide paving on an intimate scale.

Key to plants
1. *R.* 'Aimee Vibert' (Noisette Climber)
2. *R.* 'Albéric Barbier' (Rambler)
3. *R.* 'Albertine' (Rambler)
4. *R.* 'Golden Showers' (Modern Climber)
5. *Clematis macropetala* 'Maidwell Hall'
6. *R. primula* (Species)
7. *R.* 'Julia's Rose' (Large Flowered)
8. *R.* 'Penelope' (Hybrid Musk)
9. *Foeniculum vulgare* 'Giant Bronze' (bronze fennel)
10. *R.* 'Roseraie de l'Hay' (Rugosa)
11. *Lavandula angustifolia* 'Hidcote'
12. *Milium effusum* 'Aureum'
13. *Scabiosa caucasica* 'Clive Greaves'
14. *Campanula persicifolia* var. *alba*
15. *Geranium clarkei* 'Kashmir White'
16. *R.* 'Buff Beauty' (Hybrid Musk)
17. *Acanthus spinosus*
18. *R.* 'Golden Wings' (Modern Shrub)
19. *R.* × *odorata* 'Pallida' (syn. 'Old Blush China')
20. *Salvia nemorosa* 'East Friesland'
21. *Sisyrinchium striatum*
22. *Heuchera* 'Red Spangles'
23. *Viola* 'Molly Sanderson'
24. *Santolina rosmarinifolia* ssp. *rosmarinifolia* (syn. *S. virens*)
25. *Argyranthemum*
26. *Buxus sempervirens* (box)
27. *Iris pallida* 'Argentea Variegata'

5 · FOLIAGE FANCIES

Opposite: Persicaria
bistorta *'Superba' provides
small pink candle flowers
among a mass of foliage
patterns. The hellebores,
rounded ligularia, lacy
ferns and clean-cut* Hosta
*'Gold Standard' provide
contrasting textures and
shades of green.*

When planning the summer garden, many months of foliage are a design asset. Foliage forms, textures and colours need to be carefully evaluated because they will be there for a long time.

In the fullness of summer, it is the lush green foliage that launches the flower. Flowers without leaves would be a sorry sight. We expect to see rich green cushions of foliage between flower and soil, acting as frame or protector. Flowerless leaves are a familiar sight but leafless flowers are rare.

The stalwart evergreens cocoon the garden in winter. But their slightly dusty, hard-working leaves cannot compare with the brilliance of spring green. Every year we forget just how brilliantly green and new the burgeoning foliage looks, and each spring we value it afresh. Then the brown of the soil becomes concealed for nearly eight months as the greenness envelops throughout summer.

I always select for form first. Pattern, texture and colour are important, but the fundamental

*The architectural forms
of* Euphorbia characias
ssp. wulfenii *and*
Phormium tenax *'Varie-
gatum' are footed by
rounded bergenia leaves.*

The magnificent foliage around this pond includes blue and green hostas, tall flag irises, bronze rodgersia, ligularia and rheum. Primulas and trollius add a blaze of colour.

The richly dark, jagged leaves of Rodgersia podophylla *provide a strong contrast in front of the tiered, white-flowered* Viburnum plicatum 'Mariesii'.

shape of the foliage can make summer gardens exciting or bland. When choosing your plants at a garden centre do look for some large foliage plants to rest the eye amid the mass of flowers.

Architectural foliage

It is the large-leaved plants that are noticed first. Some are quite restful but others provide more dramatic shapes. The most immediately eye-catching are those with sword-like foliage. These act as the accent plants of summer. *Phormium tenax* (New Zealand flax) can easily attain 3m (9ft). *Yucca gloriosa*, which is similar but has more rigidly sharp leaves and *Cordyline australis* have the same dramatic profile. For a softer effect *Crocosmia masoniorum* is also sword-like, but because the flowers are a brilliant orange-red this will have to be considered in the planting scheme. A similarly sized *Iris pseudacorus*, the common flag iris, has the same authoritative impact, and its variegated form *I. p.* 'Variegata', with striking cream stripes, is particularly fine. Such powerfully shaped plants as these may be assembled with other sculptured forms like rounded hebes. Alternatively, some of the tall, massed herbaceous plants, like the majestic delphinium varieties or the huge *Eremurus robustus* (foxtail lily), which may make 2.4m (8ft) in the season, and the 1.8m (6ft) *Cimicifuga simplex* 'Prichard's Giant (syn. *C. ramosa*), spikes of late summer, will balance the huge leaves of *Phormium tenax*.

Sometimes 'sword' is the wrong word, as when softer strap-like leaves relax into flowing curved forms. *Hemerocallis* (day lily), *Liriope muscari* (lily-turf) and plants like *Libertia formosa* have much softer forms, which merge rather than stand out as individuals. The grasses obviously have a role to play here, but they are discussed separately later on (see pages 96–105).

Some large leaves are especially dominant. The wonderful *Rheum palmatum* proudly displays huge, reddish palmate leaves. Although it is usually grown as specimen plant, I have seen a

most successful mass planting of these beneath a spacious grove of white-barked birches. Note that rheums must not dry out. In damp conditions you could also be delighted to grow some of the attractive rodgersias. Few huge-leaved plants can cope with heat and dryness, so shade or semi-shade is often a prerequisite. The stylish *Macleaya cordata* (plume poppy) is an exception. This plant demands sun. It is very tall and wildly spreading, and has handsome, deeply lobed, palmate, grey leaves to set off its brownish-pink sprays of tiny flowers. In a fussy or texturally over-rich planting design, these foliage plants are absolutely perfect.

Some smaller plants can be surprisingly influential. Bergenias are noted for their 'elephant ears' leaves. Hostas are among the most sculpted foliage around. The woolly silvered foliage of *Stachys byzantina* (syn. *S. lanata*), should be mentioned here because, like the others, it is always noticed and has the effect of soothing an over-rich planting scheme.

Phormium tenax 'Variegatum' is always a notable architectural plant. Here it dominates the red leaves of the berberis and the blue-toned juniper.

51

Foliage mass

Not all foliage should be so presumptive. The garden would be a restless place if every plant had strong architectural form. Many shapes are fairly amorphous and add texture and colour without drawing attention to themselves. These are the mainstay of the garden, providing a stabilizing effect, and adding a fullness to the summer garden long after their own flowers are over. Among them are astilbes, heuchera, sages, spiraea, many geraniums, tiarella and epimediums. At a higher level, 60cm to 1m (2–3ft), the leaves of peonies are generously fulfilling, and many hydrangeas, such as *Hydrangea quercifolia* and *Hydrangea aspera* ssp. *sargentiana*, are themselves pretty, yet merge well with more eye-catching shrubs. At shrub height, viburnums, salix, elaeagnus, elders and cornus have similar value as mass greenery, acting as alternative backgrounds.

Ground cover Neat little ajugas, lamiums and trails of vinca complete the ground carpet. The beautifully formed, almost heart-shaped leaves of the epimedium family, suspended above the soil by thin, wiry stems, are there for eight months of the year, and a few are evergreen. In shaded acidic soils *Maianthemum bifolium, Asarum europaeum* and *Galax urceolata* (syn. *G. aphylla*) have simple leaves, while *Pachysandra terminalis* creates more decorative patterns. Above these richly carpeting foliage textures, summer flowers will show themselves to advantage: like the tall blue aconites, the grand *Cardiocrinum giganteum,* stately foxgloves, the captivating martagon lilies and the umbelliferous flowers of *Nectaroscordum siculum* ssp. *bulgaricum.*

Edging plants When considering the fringe benefits of the border, *Alchemilla mollis* (lady's mantle) and *Geranium renardii* are very pretty. Both are favoured with attractive jade green, rounded foliage, soft to touch. Multi-leaved catmint,

Nepeta racemosa (syn. *N. mussinii*), or the low grass-like forms of *Armeria* (thrift) provide low-level textures, which pleasingly edge herbaceous borders. Heucheras can perform the same function. They are close to the ground, forming rosettes of foliage that launch the clouds of flowers overhead. *Heuchera micrantha* var. *diversifolia* 'Palace Purple' has lush red-purple leaves, with pale pink flowers. There are also new greyish and silvered cultivars such as *Heuchera* 'Pewter Moon' and *H.* 'Snow Storm'.

Textured foliage

Taking the rough with the smooth, but in a positive way, will enhance the summer garden.

Contrast Coarsely textured foliage beside fragile flowers adds a piquancy to a scene. If all were continuous sweetness and light the result might be rather sickly. So consider an occasional dynamic contrast, for example, using *Viburnum rhytidophyllum,* with its leathery foliage, to back a group of the delicate *Aquilegia* (columbines). Not everyone likes the leaves of *Viburnum rhytidophyllum* as much as I do, but the notion of beauty and the beast is irresistible.

Conversely, there are sharply textured plants like *Eryngium bourgatii* (sea holly). Adjectives describe these plants as 'jagged' and 'steely blue'. Try them with a soft-texture association of *Santolina pinnata* ssp. *neapolitana* 'Sulphurea', which has a rounded, green, feathery form, and whose pale lemon flowers would coincide nicely in early summer. Eryngiums would also be flattered if they were grown in association with the velvet-textured, darkly purple leaves of a *Salvia officinalis* Purpurascens Group.

Some texture changes are very necessary to calm the overflowing chaos of summer glory. The sober ribbed leaves of the rounded *Viburnum davidii* are most effective. Frothy flowers like gypsophila or alchemilla, or the pinky haze of

Thalictrum delavayi, or even the flashing colours of the shaggy inulas, with their finely rayed petals, are all emphasized by contrast. Similarly, velvety leaved *Phlomis fruticosa* (Jerusalem sage) looks especially effective when it is grown with the crisp, linear leaves of *Euphorbia griffithii* 'Fireglow' or *E. lathyris* (caper spurge), even after the flowers have departed.

Grassy foliage is an extremely important texture in most herbaceous beds. You will notice it in many forms, either as true grasses (as described on pages 96–105), or plants that masquerade as grasses, such as *Hemerocallis* (day lilies), *Liriope spicata, Sisyrinchium striatum,* the shafts of kniphofia, iris-like leaves of libertia, or the strap leaves of the agapanthus.

Glossy light-reflecting leaves are invaluable in shade. The laurels and aucubas provide this at shrub level, but on the ground, less lustrous but still glossy, the foliage of *Asarum europaeum* has fine, rounded leaves. Consorting with polystichum ferns and their richly textured forms, the contrast is most effective.

Harmony Too much contrast can, however, be restless. Most of us are looking for tranquillity in the summer garden, and a harmony of texture is very soothing. Feathery textures work well together: astilbes are used to being with ferns; geraniums are often with alchemillas. Grassy, flowing day lily foliage is often near irises, and each flatters the other. Equally effective, woolly or velvet plants look good when sited together. Sages work with *Stachys byzantina* (lamb's tongue) and *Nepeta × faassenii* (catmint). The hostas also mix with one another despite size differences and colour contrasts, which leads me to discuss the value of foliage colour, even in high summer when you would think that the colour of flower power is all you need.

Matching blues, but very different plants. A grass,
Festuca glauca *'Elijah Blue', is grown with a conifer,*
Picea pungens *'Koster'.*

53

Opposite: Lonicera nitida *'Baggesen's Gold'* is an evergreen shrub with a dense mass of tiny leaves resembling box. Here it contrasts with the beautifully striped leaves of Iris pallida *'Variegata' (syn.* I.p. *'Aurea Variegata')* in full flower. The yellow-flowered potentilla echoes the golden leaves of the lonicera.

Mostly evergreen, these shrubs offer foliage with varied textures and colours. Ivy and juniper trail over the low wall, and grey santolina, variegated elaeagnus, thuja, cotoneaster, berberis and a Japanese maple provide the shapes and textures.

Colour in leaves

Foliage colour is almost as varied and beautiful as that of flowers.

Greens Although it is often thought of as a neutral in the garden, green is a colour in its own right, and the variety of bottle greens, lime greens, apple greens and grass greens, through to olive colours and blue-toned glaucous greens, is limitless. The dark richness of the *Prunus lusitanica* (Portuguese laurel) and *Taxus baccata* (yew) are a foil against which brighter greens, like those of many ferns, grasses and hostas, look stunning. Among such leaves, green, white and cream flowers can be very pretty. For example, *Thalictrum lucidum* carries panicles of creamy-green flowers, *Santolina rosmarinifolia* ssp. *rosmarinifolia* (syn. *S. virens*) is a mass of fine green foliage dotted with lemon yellow flowers, *Heuchera cylindrica* 'Greenfinch'

has tiny green bell flowers, and *Geranium sylvaticum* 'Album' is a wonderful pure white, set off by its matt green foliage.

Golds Golden-leaved shrubs are sometimes quite as brilliant as any flower. They are used most effectively in a yellow and blue flower border, and will last throughout the season. Grasses like the butter yellow *Carex elata* 'Aurea' (Bowles' golden sedge) or *Milium effusum* 'Aureum' add texture as well as colour. Yellow-hued hostas, such as *Hosta* 'Gold Standard', add clarity of form, while the tiny-leaved evergreen shrub *Lonicera nitida* 'Baggesen's Gold' or the flamboyant *Elaeagnus pungens* 'Maculata', provide ever-gold shrub backing. Yellow-leaved deciduous shrubs like *Philadelphus coronarius* 'Aureus', *Acer shirasawanum* f. *aureum* (syn. *A. japonicum* f. *aureum*) and *Berberis thunbergii* 'Aurea' must be given protection from the heat of the midday sun, or they will be burnt.

When yellow leans towards more orange hues, the effect with blues is bolder and more powerful than it is with the paler associations. One shrub that needs careful siting is *Spiraea japonica* 'Goldflame'. This has yellow colouring which verges on rust-orange when the leaves arrive in early summer but gradually fades to a lime green. However, sited near some of the warmer orange-based flowers such as *Euphorbia griffithii* 'Fireglow', *Kniphofia galpinii*, *Uncinia unciniata*, a brown sedge and mahogany day lilies, it is most effective.

The huge *Fraxinus excelsior* 'Jaspidea' is a wonderful ash tree provided you have space, for it is a forest-sized tree. Failing that, *Robinia pseudoacacia* 'Frisia' and *Gleditsia triacanthos* 'Sunburst' are intensely yellow-leaved trees and are manageable heights. The first is fast growing and reaches 6m (20ft), while the second is slow growing and slightly smaller.

Silvers Grey or silver foliage harmonizes with most schemes in the garden. Consider using the evergreen eucalyptus, *Eucalyptus gunnii* – a tall

Above: *The cream-edged* Hosta crispula *dominates the greys and silvers of this group.*

Velvet-leaved Stachys byzantina *(lamb's tongue) is irresistibly tactile.*

20m (65ft) – or *E. pauciflora* ssp. *niphophila* – 10m (30ft), or, on a smaller scale, the pretty *Pyrus salicifolia* 'Pendula' (weeping pear), which would suit most gardens. Some shrub willows, like *Salix daphnoides* (violet willow), or the rampantly invasive but very charming, 4m (13ft), silvery *Salix exigua* (coyote willow)*,* are very fetching and suited to large country gardens.

When you are planning a garden with silver plants as backing shrubs, *Elaeagnus commutata* is a useful greyed evergreen, and *Elaeagnus* 'Quicksilver' (syn. *E. angustifolia* Caspica Group; oleaster), although deciduous and reaching 3m (10ft), may also grace the back of the border. If you have space, the latter can also be a solo specimen, as it has extremely silvery and finely willowy foliage, which catches the light. However, it does need a lot of space, so for smaller gardens consider instead the artemisias. Their silver-grey foliage blends readily with blue and yellow borders, but they are outstandingly effective when used with white, pink and red flowers.

Silver-greys are traditionally used in rose gardens. The low-growing, 80cm (2ft 6in), *Convolvulus cneorum* is probably the silkiest of all grey foliage, quite different in texture from the furry *Stachys byzantina* 'Silver Carpet', the woolly textured, larger leaved version of lamb's ears. Both must be sited in sunny areas.

Some grey foliage has a cleaner line and harder texture. The beautiful grey-blue hostas, like the enormous *Hosta sieboldiana* var. *elegans* or the more manageable *H.* 'Blue Moon' are excellent for adding crispness. Smaller and bluer *H.* 'Halcyon' grows 45cm (1ft 6in) wide and has a more delicate appearance. These plants are very fetching with grassy textures as well as associating naturally with some of the damper astilbes, ferns and ligularias.

Some very small grey hebes add character beside paving or in raised beds. *Hebe pinguifolia* 'Pagei' and jade-grey *Hebe albicans* 'Red Edge' are neat edging shrubs, and the pretty, tiny silver foliage of *Hebe pimeliodes* 'Quicksilver' has a charming rococo effect. All are around 50–60cm (20–24in) tall.

On the whole, the smaller of the grey-leaved plants should be massed. Avoid a 'dotted' effect of solo planting, and let the plants weave in and out of others.

Reds Some grey leaves are overlaid with reddish hues, in particular *Rosa glauca* (syn. *R. rubrifolia*) and *Cotinus* 'Grace' with their wine-coloured tinge. *Cotinus coggygria* 'Royal Purple' is, on the other hand, truly claret red and looks magnificent with grey-leaved *Verbascum bombyciferum*, the very silvered, woolly biennial, even when the yellow flowers appear. The acers are important here, particularly *Acer palmatum* 'Bloodgood' or *A. palmatum* f. *atropurpureum*. *Berberis thunbergii* f. *atropurpurea* is another dark red-leaved shrub; it requires a lot of space but is easy to prune. *Phormium tenax* Purpureum Group offers deeply red sword leaves, which have great dramatic presence among the herbaceous red flowers and may be useful for adding a dark or warmer tone. Mix red foliage with scarlet and crimson summer flowers, such as vermilion lobelia, deep red astilbes, orange-red crocosmia and rusty heleniums. Later, red penstemons make a bold, powerful planting. You could even add *Veratrum nigrum*. Red borders are not easy. However, there is much fun to be had.

Strongly coloured red foliage is provided by the shrub Berberis thunbergii *'Bagatelle'.*

DESIGN FOR A FOLIAGE BORDER

In a large garden a border such as this would be simple to maintain yet be a joy for much of the year because the plants have been selected for their foliage. Throughout the whole of the summer in particular there will be changes in shape, texture and colour. As a bonus, flowers add piquancy, changing the emphasis as the season progresses, but it is the leaves that provide continuous rich patterns, lush and rewarding for many months from spring onwards.

The border is dominated by two similar, distinctive ornamental trees. The taller one, *Aralia elata* 'Variegata', has huge, doubly pinnate leaves, which float above this multi-stemmed plant. Known also as the Japanese angelica tree, this is really a shrub, but the habit is usually sparse because prickly stems rise from the ground as suckers, supporting the magnificent foliage and creating a tree-like canopy. Usually about 5m (16ft) tall, it can sometimes reach as much as 9m (over 30ft). The spectacular variegated leaves, often 90cm (3ft) long, grow in a ruff around the

central stem. Despite their size they are light and delicate, with creamy white variegation. By late summer creamy, lace-like, billowing flower panicles trail beneath the foliage in perfect accord. This is a remarkably beautiful plant.

At the other end of the bed *Rhus typhina*, the stag's horn sumach, echoes the foliage pattern of the aralia but has quite different qualities. The thick branching stems are not prickly but are covered with a dark brown velvet. The leaves are as long as those of the aralia and are pinnate, but they are dark green and serrated, and in late summer they begin to colour to a flamed scarlet. This plant is more of a tree, and it can reach 5m (15ft). The canopy creates more shade beneath it, so is underplanted here with ferns and hellebores and edged with liriope (lilyturf) where the border faces the sun. The image is heavier than that of the aralia, and this is further emphasized in autumn, when stiffly erect seedheads occur on the female plants. A more delicate form is *R. t.* 'Dissecta' (syn. *R. t.* 'Laciniata').

These two spectacularly foliaged plant dominate the bed throughout summer, but evergreens support the group during the whole year. *Olearia × macrodonta* (New Zealand holly) has aromatic grey-green leaves and in early

Flag irises have tall, slim, reed-like leaves virtually perpendicular to the surface of the water.

Key to plants
1. *Aralia elata* 'Variegata'
2. *Epimedium grandiflorum* 'Rose Queen'
3. *Bergenia ciliata*
4. *Iris foetidissima* var. *citrina*
5. *Hosta* 'Green Fountain'
6. *Cotinus coggygria* 'Notcutt's Variety'
7. *Olearia × macrodonta*
8. *Macleaya cordata* 'Flamingo'
9. *Cimicifuga simplex* 'Brunette'
10. *Artemisia ludoviciana* 'Silver Queen'
11. *Sisyrinchium striatum* var. *variegatum* (sun. *S. s.* 'Aunt May')
12. *Santolina rosmarinifolia* ssp. *rosmarinifolia* (syn. *S. virens*) 'Primrose Gem'
13. *Hemerocallis citrina*
14. *Lupinus arboreus*
15. *Paeonia delavayi* var. *ludlowii* (syn. *P. lutea* var. *ludlowii*)
16. *Viburnum davidii*
17. *Helleborus foetidus* Wester Flisk Group
18. *Liriope muscari*
19. *Polystichum setiferum*
20. *Rhus typhina*

summer bears masses of white daisy flowers. It is not a holly at all, but it does have prickly leaves and grows to a height of 6m (20ft) by 5m (15ft). *Viburnum davidii* is lower growing, forming neat domes of about 1.2m (4ft) by 1.5m (5ft), with beautifully structured, glossy green leaves and, if a male and female are grown, attractive blue berries in autum. These are the evergreen shrubs, and the bergenias, epimediums and ferns and the grass-like leaves of iris, liriope and sisyrinchium provide herbaceous, semi-green backing as well.

Through the months of summer deciduous plants create new forms and detailed patterns. *Hemerocallis*, commonly known as day lilies, lengthen the drift of grass-like leaves. Adding the luxuriant foliage of tall tree peonies and the fast-growing, generous sprawl of textures provided by tree lupins creates a wealth of contrasting greenery. Among this, stately *Macleaya cordata* forms simpler shapes. Although quickly spreading, it responds to creative weeding. This is a tall peren-nial – 1.5m (5ft) – valued for its large, rounded and lobed grey leaves. The colour echoes the foliage of the olearia behind and is further empha-sized by the silvery artemisia to the front. In contrast, a large mass of wine red cotinus foliage backs these silver-greys, linking with the bronze-red leaves of the late-summer-flowering cimicifuga.

As always, however, it is the richness of the greens that binds the summer foliage scheme together, and this is provided by the grassy leaved plants, by the velvet emerald of the santolina, the overlapping hostas, the lacy ferns and the low-growing, ground-covering bergenias and epimediums.

The lavish summer foliage provides a constant and vital border, within which flowers come and go, altering and enhancing the picture as the season progresses.

Different hostas, Hosta sieboldiana *var.* elegans *and* H. fortunei *var.* albopicta, *merge with* Meconopsis cambrica *(Welsh poppy), yellow trollius and lime green milium grass.*

61

6 • PERENNIALS ABLAZE

Opposite: *Mixed tall perennials, backed by* Macleaya cordata, *include a golden inula and a deep blue aconite, with some phlox at the front.*

This is what the summer garden is truly about. All other seasons have charm and affect mood; the arts often use the seasons to create the pervading spirit of their work, but whereas spring is the season for stirring optimism, summer is considered the time of tranquillity. The build-up of spring-flowering shrubs and bulbs, so welcome at the time, is easily forgotten in the largesse of summer.

Thoughtful planning is needed to ensure that the season gradually evolves from the yellows and blues of late winter bulbs, through the pink and white blossom of early spring, to the effulgence of herbaceous plants in the summer garden. Then, every shade, colour, texture and form create the lush summer tapestry. As one flower association fades there is another to take its place, so the patterns and colours are rarely the same from week to week. To prepare for this, the gardener needs to know when flowers reach their peak, and which stalwarts will overlap month on month. I have

Mixed perennials in all the glory of summer acquire luminous colouring in evening light. The small tree Gleditsia triacanthos 'Sunburst' *provides yellow foliage behind borders that include poppies, asphodels, sisyrinchium, irises and rheum.*

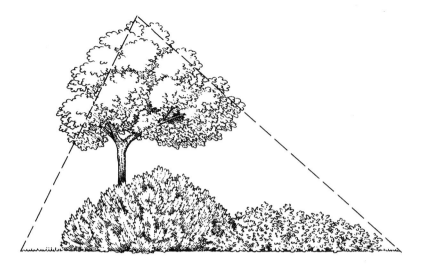

Fig. 1

Fig. 3

Fig. 2

therefore outlined three periods of the summer season – early, mid- and late – describing the flowers as they reach their zenith at these times.

I will assume that the soils are a neutral loam. If you are now gnashing your teeth over your thinly covered chalk garden, or if you work with cold clay, which has either the consistency of chewing gum or fractured concrete, consult a good reference book with the aim of improving your particular soil.

Two plans are included in the chapter. Both are basically perennial borders, but include some shrubs. The designs were planned with distinctive colour schemes, associating either cool colours or hot colours. But in both borders there is also great variety of texture, form and shape.

GROUPING FOR HEIGHT AND FORM

The fundamental success of any planting scheme depends on a recognition that plants have distinctive shapes and that there are spaces between them. Grouping plants so that one is dominant and the others build around it in triangular form is a simple device, often used and very effective. Fig. 1 illustrates this. Alternatively, the main focal plant may be particularly graceful, like the Japanese maples, in which case it is necessary to surround it with low plants to allow it space to display. Fig. 2 shows this and includes a small form as a balance. Herbaceous plant groups may be developed in just the same way, as seen in Fig. 3. Note that in this case, the smallest plants duplicate the form of the main one. This kind of composition is appropriate for all sizes of plant. It relies on the recognition that many plants have a distinctive form.

Some are extremely dominant – the 'prima donnas'. The biennial *Onopordum acanthium*, a branching silver wrongly named Scotch thistle, is 2m (6ft) high, and *Eremurus robustus* (foxtail lily) at 1.5m (5ft) are examples. Plants like these add excitement to a scheme and provide a visual focus.

Prima donnas may be giant shapes, wide shapes or distinctive verticals. They always catch the eye.

Then there is a second rank in the authoritative role, in which plants like irises, lythrums and lupins have vertical and eye-catching form. Photograph any well-balanced herbaceous bed with a black and white film and these forms will be very evident, making the bed attractive even without colour.

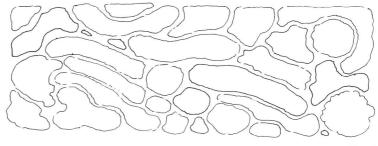

Fig. 4

LAYOUT

The tallest border plants do not necessarily have to go at the back of the border. Such logical regimentation denies the natural fluidity of plant growth. Overlapping and interweaving forms create much more harmonious images. Gertrude Jekyll often employed diagonally meandering plant masses. The borders she describes were often deeper and larger than our more modest sites, but the principles are the same.

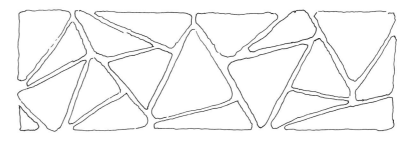

Fig. 5

Planting drifts

Grouping is the essential by which unnatural linear regimentation can be avoided. Massing plants is so much more effective than dotting them, and the patterns that emulate nature by creating flows of plants are very attractive. These can then be enlivened with a few spectacular subjects.

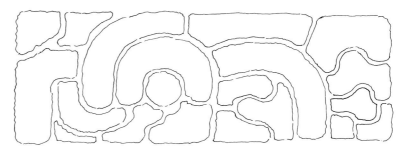

Fig. 6

Plant masses may be grouped in many different ways – the flowing lines of Jekyll's plant association, meandering forms (Fig. 4), interlocking, roughly triangular forms or enclosed areas (Fig. 5).

People tend to move through a garden, so as one progresses along the border, there should be hidden surprises and changing rhythms. The relationships between plants are rarely static, unless one is dealing with yuccas or opuntias.

Large and striking plants do not always have to be at the back. They could come forward towards the spectator, creating a three-dimensional mass and breaking up the mid-height and lower planting patterns.

It is also interesting to think about creating 'wave-lengths' of planting patterns, where some colours may crush together densely, while others stretch out into larger slackened masses. This makes for rhythm and movement, and will add drama to an arrangement.

Another way of grouping plants is to form pockets, where major plants enclose smaller ones (Fig. 6). This would be less dynamic than the scheme above, but very charming as one passes along a border. Here again, opportunities will occur for using dominant shapes with gentler patterns. Within this type of scheme, colour contrast or harmonies may alter along the border.

Colour power

Strong or dark colour may be used as a foil to delicate pastels or as a control to more vibrant tints. For example, both *Lobelia* 'Dark Crusader' and *L.* 'Queen Victoria', with their dark plum leaves and 80cm (2ft 8in) columns of brilliant scarlet flowers, are very noticable, as, later on, is the deep plum-brown leaved *Cimicifuga simplex* 'Prichard's Giant' (syn. *C. ramosa*) with its elegant white flower spikes up to 2.1m (7ft).

On the other hand, colour itself may be the *raison d'être* of the plan. Planning a restricted palette is a device used by many leading designers. As a result, one sees red borders, yellow borders and the appealing romantic 'silver' borders. By these methods, selection is partially controlled. Those with flair, however, can also use with effect the odd 'mishap'. Such 'errors' occur in the wild, where an oddity, possibly darker, brighter or of a different scale or form, may be thrown up. In one's

Above: *Yellow is the theme that links this garden in summer. Plants such as holly, yew, ivy and berberis provide the structure for perennials for the three phases of summer.*

Right: *Strong pinks merge into shades of orange and ruby red. Clipped evergreen forms unite the design.*

own plan, to 'throw' an unlikely burnt orange colour into a sea of blues and purples could be as powerful as adding a spiky form to an otherwise mellow border of soft textures.

Summery colours strongly favour yellows, ranging from cream, through primrose, cadmium and ochre into oranges and browns. Such a border could contain pale 'moonlight' achilleas, *Coreopsis verticillata* 'Moonbeam' or *Scabiosa columbaria* var. *ochroleuca*, all three of which have pale lemon flowers. In addition, pure yellow *Oenothera biennis* (evening primrose), the day lily *Hemerocallis* 'Stella de Oro' and the buttercup yellow *Ranunculus acris* 'Flore Pleno' will intensify the colour. Then the rich yellows of the rudbeckias, *Solidago* 'Cloth of Gold' (golden rod), *Heliopsis helianthoides* 'Gigantea' and *Helenium* 'Wyndley' begin quite clearly to lean towards the oranges, *Crocosmia* 'Lady Hamilton' is clearly halfway between both yellow and orange.

Similar schemes may be planned, working through the blues, from turquoise to near purple, or the reds, from maroon through to orange. Thus the theme of a border could be undertaken with this spectrum approach in mind. The result will be highly controlled, but it may be rather sterile unless you introduce some unexpected contrasts. It is up to you.

Early summer

To establish a link between late spring and early summer introduce some shrubs, like tree peonies and Japanese maples, to create wonderful leafy background. Many of the tree peonies have magnificent flowers, and the foliage is also quite outstanding. *Paeonia delavayi* and *P. delavayi* var. *lutea* in particular have magnificent leaves.

The foliage of the Japanese acers is smaller but no less beautiful, and it is exquisitely decorative when surrounded by other foliage plants.

Cream, yellow and white are the theme of this scheme, which features Sisyrinchium striatum, Geranium sylvaticum *'Album' and the tufted hair grass,* Deschampsia caespitosa *'Bronzeschleier' (syn. 'Bronze Veil'), with yellow flag irises planted behind.*

Form and shape in early summer When you are establishing plant associates, remember that the shapes of the plants help to hold the design together, and here the verticals are especially important. Early on, plants like the tall hybrid *Kniphofia* 'Atlanta', a flaming orange-red spike of 1.2m (4ft), the cream flowering *Sisyrinchium striatum* and *Asphodelus albus*, which, at 1m (3ft), is very distinctive because the brown calyx on the single stem reveals white flowers, are dominant, because they have thrusting profiles. In the same month the stately *Asphodeline lutea*, although 30cm (12in) shorter, is nevertheless so striking that its common name, king's spear, tells all.

Cultivars of *Anchusa azurea* will also provide good verticals. The tall, rich blue flowers cannot fail to catch the eye when grouped in a herbaceous border, and they would be most fetching with the early-flowering day lily *Hemerocallis lilioasphodelus* (syn. *H. flava*). The white *Anthericum liliago* var. *major* is an elegant aristocrat about 1m (3ft) high, best planted in threes or fives, and a dense planting of the grassy-leaved *Libertia formosa* among them would flatter these attractive flowers. The superb *Ostrowskia magnifica* will produce large, blue, bell-shaped flowers above bluish leaves up to 1.5m (5ft) high, given a warm situation.

In early summer the creamy *Camassia leichtlinii* 'Plena' has flower spikes holding starry flowers from base to tip, reaching a height of nearly 1.2m (4ft). Camassias are summer-flowering bulbs and may be used either as informal plants for naturalizing or in the more organized border.

To the tall flowering plants of early summer I must add the iris. There are irises for almost any part of the growing season, and although the

Intensely red dahlias and velvety red phlox add depth to a hot colour scheme, combining with yellow solidago and helenium. At the back is the apricot-coloured rose R. 'Golden Years'.

69

Iris 'Blue Rythm' complements the orange flowers of geum within a border of herbaceous plants and shrubs.

lovely dwarf bearded irises are finished by early summer, the true iris flower of the original *fleur de lys* may be found, as summer begins, in the *germanica* strains. The *innominata* hybrids and the *pallida* forms are also early.

The simplicity of the foliage of the lovely *Iris pallida,* which grows to 80cm (32in), is valuable, as is the grey-white cultivar 'Argentea Variegata', with its fans of variegated foliage. Planted in repetitive patterns, the leaves will last summer through. A yellow variegation in the leaf, now called *I.*

pallida 'Variegata', is also charming but the slim *I. pseudacorus* 'Variegata' is very much taller, growing to 2m (6ft) and very dominant, although it is less fan-shaped than others.

There are other herbaceous plants that certainly intend to be noticed. The remarkably shaped *Crambe cordifolia* (giant sea kale), which produces huge, rounded, dark green cabbage leaves, covers an area of 2 × 2m (6 × 6ft) when fully developed. A large site is obviously important, and, unusually for large-leaved plants, it is able to grow in full sun.

Left: *Massed in the fore-ground, warm orange* Euphorbia griffithii *relates visually to the colour of the copper beech in the distance.*

Below: *A midsummer group, dominated by white valerian, has silvery* Stachys byzantina *'Cotton Ball' below and massed* Thalictrum flavum *ssp.* glaucum *(syn.* T. speciosissimum*) planted behind.*

During early summer this magnificent monster brings forth clouds of delicate and light-hearted white flowers on long branching stems.

Its smaller relative is far more compact and has delicate, blue-lobed foliage. This is the blue *Crambe maritima* (sea kale). When massed together, these plants would be striking with the burnt orange of *Euphorbia griffithii* 'Fireglow'.

For grey foliage and fluffy flowers the earliest of the meadow rues, *Thalictrum aquilegiifolium*, is an asset to a planting scheme. The flowers reach approximately 1m (3ft) as a deliciously hazy pink-lilac mass above the leaves, which are reminiscent of columbine. Because it flowers at the same time as the *Papaver orientale* (oriental poppy), the contrast between the simple flower shape of the poppy and that of the fluffy thalictrum is most effective. If these plants were linked by a ground planting of *Geranium renardii*, with its neat, downy, sage green leaves and violet-veined white flowers, the result would be coolly charming.

Like their siblings the tree peonies, the early herbaceous peonies provide lush foliage for much of the season, as well as flowers. The exquisite spring-flowering species peonies are followed shortly by the cottage garden favourite, the double red *Paeonia officinalis* 'Rubra Plena', and then the beautiful *Paeonia lactiflora* group comes into its own. Many are double-flowered extravagances, positively exotic when compared with most of the flowers on the early summer scene, but the old single white *P. l.* 'Whitleyi Major' has much to commend it.

Silver-grey foliage is always a flattering companion for peonies. *Stachys byzantina*, with its velvety silver leaves, reaches 60cm (24in). It and the slightly taller *Artemisia ludoviciana* 'Silver Queen' would be an impressive inclusion here.

Flower colour in early summer

Many of the less flamboyant perennials of early summer have most attractive colours and foliage textures. Once the dramatic or distinctive forms are in place, choosing flowers for their similar or contrasting colours means deciding whether to stay within a theme of 'cool' or 'hot' tones or whether to keep to pale luminous pastels. I would suggest that summer's glory is that of gaiety and that the all-pastel theme is better deployed as a smaller, though delightful part of the scheme, or incorporated as 'cooling areas' among the highly coloured border.

A backing of the brown-leaved shrub *Corylus maxima* 'Purpurea' and some pale yellow broom *Cytisus × kewensis* or massed low gold *Cytisus × beanii* would go well with yellow and red *Aquilegia formosa*. The first flowers of *Geum* 'Borisii' or *Geum* 'Coppertone' pick up with an orange theme. Some cooler yellows like *Potentilla atrosanguinea*

A reliable and invaluable perennial, Geum 'Borisii' has cheerful orange flowers throughout summer.

var. *argyrophylla,* with its silvery leaves, would be good, and *Heuchera micrantha* var. *diversifolia* 'Palace Purple', with its red leaves, would set off the scene well.

The greenish flowers of the wonderful winter hellebores stay around for a long time. *Heuchera* 'Green Ivory' could pick up the greenish theme. A touch of pink from *Heucherella alba* 'Bridget Bloom' or the ivy-leaved *Heuchera americana*, with its brown-tinged green flowers, would create a pretty plant association of greens.

If you are contemplating silver foliage as the foundation of a pastel colour theme, the 30cm (12in) high *Anthemis punctata* ssp. *cupaniana* will be in the throes of amassing its white daisies, and blend in well. Remember, too, the extremely silvered, low-growing *Artemisia schmidtiana* 'Nana', which catches the sunlight. Beside these, a dark purple form of *Salvia officinalis* would add rich contrast. The 45cm (18in) *Geranium × oxonianum* 'Wargrave Pink' has commenced its summer-long season, and the rich deep green grassy leaves of the compact *Armeria maritima* or *A. m.*'Alba' also throw up pink or white flowers to 30cm (12in). Pale yellow achilleas will be starting, and aquilegias carry a great variety of gentle pastels plus some rich blue and purple colours. All have pretty glaucous foliage. Violas like *V.* 'Moonlight', with pale yellow flowers, mix well with the lilac-blue nepeta, early campanulas and dicentras.

As indispensable in early summer as the dicentras, the perennial wallflower *Erysimum* 'Bowles' Mauve' starts early and will add lilac-purple flower spikes up to 90cm (3ft) above ground-level greyish foliage, and continues to flower all summer.

Midsummer

As we saw in Shrubs for Structure, decorative shrubs provide invaluable shape and form. In high summer plants like fuchsias, escallonias, hibiscus, ceanothus, hebes, eucryphia, myrtus, hydrangea and lavatera have a range of colour and foliage to work with any scheme. Many of them contribute luscious fragrance as well.

Form and shape in midsummer It is again worthwhile starting with the more dominant architecturally formed plants.

Hybrid delphiniums can be absolute giants. *Delphinium* 'Crown Jewel', a towering column of mauve-blue, will actually reach 2.8m (9ft). Support is essential in case of summer storms. More modest heights of 1.5m (5ft) are, of course, available, but must still be staked. In addition, provide a little lime if the soil is acidic and, whatever your views on ecology, you may have to compromise over slugs.

I do not care for the recent introduction of red delphiniums. However, there are some very delicately tinted cream colours that are attractive, and the belladonna hybrids are more fragilely open-structured than the mighty cultivars. The white spires of *Epilobium angustifolium* at a mere 1.2m (4ft) or the creamy inflorescence of *Artemisia lactiflora*, reaching to about 1.8m (6ft), would create slightly different but still flattering effects with delphiniums.

Ferula communis (giant fennel) at 2m (7ft) is another possible associate, particularly with the richer blue-purples, as it carries yellow umbels above fine foliage. The tall yellow spikes of the ligularias would echo the form of the delphiniums but in a damper border.

Separated, but linked visually with delphiniums, the huge, dangerously spiked, silvered biennial *Onopordum acanthium* is equally impressive. There are some big verbascums, such as the very tall biennial *V. bombyciferum* and *V. olympicum*, or the beautiful but smaller – 60cm (24in) – hybrid *V.* 'Helen Johnson', which is in flower for a long time, its felt-like silver foliage supporting a soft copper-pink flower, and the neat *V. chaixii* forms.

The tall annual hollyhocks are wonderful fillers when other plants, such as *Papaver orientale*, have retired below soil level. They associate well with another dramatic summer perennial, *Cynara cardunculus* (cardoon), which has deeply divided silver leaves and huge purple thistle heads at about 1.8m (6ft). This is a true prima donna, which needs fairly low plants in the immediate vicinity. The cool grey leaves could be emphasized with *Achillea* 'Taygetea', with its flat heads of lemon flowers and neat silver leaves, which is only 45cm (18in) high, or *Helichrysum* 'Sulphur Light' (syn. 'Schweffellicht'), slightly smaller at 30cm (12in), which also has cool pale yellow flowers but with soft silver-grey foliage.

Cynara cardunculus *shows that herbaceous perennials are not grown just for their flowers.*

Flower colour in midsummer Pinks, whites and reds always go well with silver foliage. *Romneya coulteri* (Californian tree poppy) is another superb silver-blue perennial, but it has large white crinkled poppy flowers with yellow stamens for several weeks. It must be protected in harsh climates but is well worth the trouble. It reaches 1.2–1.5m (4–5ft) tall with a spread of 1m (3ft) in midsummer, and the flowers are scented. Pink *Sidalcea malviflora* 'Rose Queen' sited nearby will also display for weeks, as will the remarkable wine-coloured *Astrantia major* 'Hadspen Blood' at about 80cm (32in). *Monarda* 'Beauty of Cobham', a bergamot, has very pale pink petals contrasting with dark purplish calyces, and these plants would take the relationship on into late summer. The small-leaved variegated mint, *Mentha suaveolens* 'Variegata', picks up the pink-grey theme.

Allium christophii *looks wonderful with* Nepeta racemosa *(syn.* N. mussini*),* Dianthus *'Rose de Mai' and* Rosa *'Madame Lauriol de Barny'.*

But what about the yellows that are so summery? Of all the perennials that shout of summer, the cone flower or black-eyed Susan, *Rudbeckia fulgida*, is the leader. The flowers have sun-ray petals, which very slightly drop back from the rounded centres. These black centres survive prominently on the stem through winter. Rudbeckias are reliable and hardy, flowering for three or four months. A swathe of them in the summer garden, supported by similarly long-flowering *Salvia* × *sylvestris* 'May Night' (syn. 'Mainacht'), with its intense purple-blue spikes at 1m (3ft), is a striking plant. Grey-leaved *Salvia lavandulifolia* would also be a good companion. The richly brown-red leaves of *Phormium* 'Bronze Baby' (which must have winter protection) could be added in groups. Try the lighter yellow *Hemerocallis* 'Marion Vaughn' to add vitality to the colour scheme and a sweeping background of maiden grass, *Miscanthus sinensis* 'Gracillimus', plus a foreground creep of Japanese blood grass, *Imperata cylindrica* 'Red Baron'.

Ligularias are very fine, but they must have moisture-retentive soil, so the company they keep is unlikely to be those grey-foliaged plants of arid conditions. Blue hostas, on the other hand, will grow beside ligularias, and *Alchemilla mollis* will also cope in soil that is lightly damp. The pretty primrose-yellow *Cephalaria gigantea*, with its scabious flowers, will provide dots of colour up to 2m (7ft) throughout the summer if it is growing in moist earth, and white-flowering astilbes would harmonize with the composition.

There are many midsummer herbaceous plants that are softly coloured and drift around one another. Notice that some, like achilleas and some daisy flowers, are quite 'flat-headed', whereas others, like penstemons, sisyrinchium and liriope, create vertical rhythmic patterns.

Silver foliage plants relate to all schemes, so *Tanacetum densum* will provide tiny, 15cm (6in) high, silvery patterns in the front of the border, and for company, use the smaller geraniums like the very pale pink *Geranium × cantabrigiensis* 'Biokovo', which grows to 20cm (8in), or the richer pink *Geranium cinereum* 'Ballerina', which is half the height. For flowering silver plants, *Anthemis punctata* ssp. *cupaniana,* at 30cm (12in), has white daisies that will continue to flower if regularly dead-headed, and *Anaphalis margaritacea* carries darker grey leaves completed with white clusters of 'everlasting' smaller daisies.

If the rose-pink, 35cm (14in) high, *Diascia rigescens* is high on your list of priorities, then a little silver nestling to accompany it would be appropriate – *Artemisia schmidtiana* 'Nana', which is only 10cm (4in) high, for example. Enlarge this scheme to include *Dictamnus albus,* with its lily-like white flowers 1m (3ft) tall, and a group of *Astrantia major* ssp. *involucrata*, which is 80cm (32in) high and has wonderful shaggy pale pink flowers.

Add texture to the above with the steel blue teasels of *Eryngium bourgatii* 'Forncett Ultra' at 60cm (24in) or *Eryngium variifolium* at 45cm (18in), with its exceptional whiteness and jagged form.

Late summer

By late summer the colours are beginning to change, but there are still plenty of new flowers around. The hydrangeas are now in full blast, some buddleias are still in flower, many escallonias are at their best, and potentillas like the pale yellow *P. fruticosa* 'Elizabeth' are still taking part. On acid soil, the beautiful *Eucryphia glutinosa* produces its exquisite white flowers. Many fuchsias are packed with colour, and at a lower level, blues become available with perovskia, caryopteris and ceratostigma. But, if they are allowed to, the marshmallow pink lavateras may well dominate the late summer scene.

Shape and form in late summer Here again I shall deal with the larger plants first. The huge *Cimicifuga simplex* 'Prichard's Giant' has erect white flower spikes, which attain 2.1m (7ft) at the end of

summer. The smaller *C. simplex* 'White Pearl' is softer, having a more arching habit and, when massed, these creamy wands above a sea of green foliage are most fetching. All the cimicifugas have an elegant habit. With these, the pale blue flowers of the monkshood, *Aconitum carmichaelii* – a plant of vertical habit and grace – make a pretty contrast and reach 1.2m (4ft). Do note that the roots of aconites are poisonous, but many plants can create problems if gardeners are not thorough when cleaning their hands.

Kniphofias are still providing their dominant stiff columns of flowers in colours from red to orange and yellow. *K.* 'Toasted Corn' and *K.* 'Apricot Souffle' indicate the range.

Texture as well as colour provide drama when mixing perennials. The silvery but spiky eryngiums contrast with deep blue campanulas.

Late-summer colour is seen here beneath a burgeoning apple tree.

The pink nerine and the Kaffir lilies (*Schizostylis*) are rather more elegant in their characteristic forms.

Colour in late summer There are many pinks around towards the end of the year. The Japanese anemones become the stars of the garden, having provided ground-covering foliage through the summer. *Anemone × hybrida* cultivars will reach 60cm (24in) to 90cm (36in) in height, and will grow in sun or shade. They come in a variety of pinks and also in white.

In the same colour range, but dependent on a warm season and a lot of sun, is the perfection of the flowering bulb, *Nerine bowdenii*, a South African native with exotic lily flowers. These, too, come in a range of pinks, reaching just over 30cm (12in), and continue to flower through into early autumn.

Both Japanese anemones and nerines will benefit from a mass of *Sedum* 'Herbstfreude' (syn. 'Autumn Joy'). This reliable old plant provides neat jade green foliage through the season, then flat, dense flower heads, which begin pink and quickly turn to a coppery claret red by late summer. This rich velvet-effect colour lasts well into the autumn.

The flowers of *Sedum spurium* 'Atropurpureum' are reddish, but as they age they become bronzed. This touch of yellow in the base tint of the colour suggests to me different colour associations. In full sun *Phygelius × rectus* 'Winchester Fanfare', with its scarlet hanging tubular flowers, brings a much warmer glow to the garden. Plant it with fresh greens like *Hosta* 'Green Fountain' or *Hosta plantaginea* var. *grandiflora*. Both of these will stand full sun and are not remotely glaucous. Just be sure that the soil will not dry out.

Hot colours are still very evident in late summer and anticipate the warmth of autumn shades. The red-leaved berberis and cotinus are considering changing to warmer rusts. A sneezeweed, *Helenium* 'Kupfersprudel' (syn. 'Copper Spray') is coloured as its name suggests. Many of the heleniums are valuable in late summer.

Green bell flowers, like those of *Galtonia viridiflora* or *G. princeps,* with their strap-like leaves, would also work with these plants. They are late summer-flowering bulbs. Elegantly tall, reaching 1.2m (4ft), they flower from midsummer into this late period, as do the agapanthus. This African lily varies from light to midnight blues, and the white *A.* 'Bressingham White' carries the same superb lily flowers.

Very late in the year, the Kaffir lilies, *Schizostylis coccinea*, are worth the wait, and will continue through into autumn. *S. c.* 'Major' is the familiar red and is 60cm (24in) tall.

Many of the late-flowering lobelias create intense effects, being vivid red combined with dark maroon leaves. Both *L.* 'Dark Crusader' and *L.* 'Queen Victoria' create rich vertical red patterns, being about 80cm (32in) tall. Provide gentle contrast with hostas as associates in moist ground. *Hosta* 'Snowden' has pointed grey-green leaves with late white flowers.

As regards ground cover, the raspberry pink *Persicaria milletii* is one of the many polygonums (persicarias) still flowering late in the season. Some are quite big, like the 1m (3ft) *P. amplexicaulis* 'Atrosanguinea', and others, neater with short flower spikes, as seen in the tiny perfection of *P. vacciniifolia.* These plants are also useful edgers, and many of them also have foliage that turns to russet brown as autumn advances.

But this is the time of year when the asters and chrysanthemums (which are now classified as *Dendranthema*) come into their own. *Aster amellus* cultivars are not troubled by mildew. *A. × frikartii* 'Mönch' is probably the finest Michaelmas daisy, with 1m (3ft) tall lavender flowers for many weeks. The shorter *A. novi-belgii* series have many reliable cultivars, and from New England *A. noviae-angliae* are also trouble free. *A. n-a.* 'Lye End Beauty' is a very tall, lavender-coloured perennial. For edging, *A. thomsonii* 'Nanus' is particularly welcome, as the leaves are greyish and the light blue flowers continue for months.

Far taller than these, the white *Chrysanthemum uliginosum* reaches 2m (7ft). It has now been renamed *Leucanthemella serotina*. By late summer the tall white daisies are very welcome as they recharge the batteries of the garden scene; they are substantial enough to grow among shrubs, particularly the sombre evergreens.

Dendranthema cultivars like the quill-petalled faded pink *D.* 'Emperor of China' and the pompon-flowered *D.* 'Bunty', the bronze *D.* 'Duchess of Edinburgh' and yellow-bronze *D.* 'Mary Stoker' are justifiably loved at the turn of the year. None of the colours is crude, and they all work well together, having little need of associates.

Dahlias are a different story. Highly exotic, the lush flowers may be 30cm (12in) in diameter, or they can be grown in small groups of hard-textured pompons. The colour range is considerable, and they look better left to themselves. Most need lifting before the frosts and planting out again in warm spring.

All season

This chapter has divided the summer season into three. Of course, it is not quite so simple. The weather may well alter the periodicity of the flowers, many overlap the months, and some, like the geranium family, have continuity of flower. Evergreens such as *Anthemis tinctoria*, dianthus, helichrysum, lavender, santolina, the sages and thymes will help to maintain the green or grey foliage, while herbaceous perennials with coloured leaves, like hostas, anaphalis, echinops and heuchera, can be used to continue the colour themes.

To fill the gaps that appear in summer, have available some summer-flowering lilies in containers, or annuals or half-hardy plants still in their pots. Remember too that the 'ten minutes of fame' allocated to a flower does not mean that the whole plant is worthless for the rest of the time. One only has to look at peonies to see that.

Left: *This glowing red border, seen in late summer, is dominated by a mature red berberis, with* Sedum spurium *'Atropurpureum', penstemon and crocosmia as permanent plants. Annuals, such as verbena, nicotiana, and amaranthus, with its red velvet spikes, contribute to the dramatic scheme.*

Below: *To the right of the path is a sweep of mauve* Verbena bonariensis, *linking with blue agapanthus, red dahlias, plum-purple hollyhocks and* Clematis viticella. *There is some effective infilling of annual nasturtiums.*

DESIGN FOR A BORDER IN COOL COLOURS

This sunny, mixed border contains mostly herbaceous plants and is 2.4m (8ft) deep by 12m (40ft) wide. It is a bed for perennials, but a few shrubs are included as foundation plants. Plants with larger mass like the rosemary, romneya, syringa, cynara and lavatera should be sited first, then those with dominant form, like the eryngium and delphinium. It is then quite simple to fill in with drifts of the smaller groups.

Good cultivation, producing weed-free soil, repays later. Prepare the ground during the previous summer by turning it over to remove perennial weeds. The soil would then be ready for autumn planting when it is still warm rather than cold and wet. Alternatively, if the soil is a heavy clay, it will be too hard to dig deeply in summer,

Cream Iris *'Langport Star' contrasts delicately with the more dominant* Eremurus himalaicus. *At the back are the gentler flowers of* Abutilon vitifolium.

so wait for autumn rains and winter frosts to make it workable. Planting can then be carried out in spring. Dig over the bed, incorporating well-rotted manure or compost and a general fertilizer.

Choose plants that are suited to the climate and soil. Some flowers need staking, while others remain upright through wind and rain. This scheme is gently cool, and the plant masses drift in linear sweeps. Silvery-grey foliage, like that of the romneya, stachys, artemisia and cynara, provides backing through the summer, and green textures like the santolina, armeria and geraniums are restful, linking the powder blues, creams, pinks, lilacs and whites of the flowers. Pin-points of wine red and deep blue add spice.

Key to plants

1. *Rosmarinus officinalis* 'Miss Jessopp's Upright'
2. *Santolina rosmarinifolia* ssp. *rosmarinifolia* (syn. *S. virens*)
3. *Aconitum carmichaelii* 'Arendsii' (monkshood)
4. *Knautia macedonica*
5. *Clematis viticella* 'Etoile Violette'
6. *Scabiosa columbaria* var. *ochroleuca*
7. *Armeria maritima* 'Alba' (thrift)
8. *Romneya coulteri* (Californian tree poppy)
9. *Caryopteris* × *clandonensis* 'Heavenly Blue'
10. *Heuchera cylindrica* 'Greenfinch'
11. *Eryngium* × *oliverianum* (sea holly)
12. *Thalictrum aquilegiifolium*
13. *Geranium pratense* 'Mrs Kendall Clark'
14. *Achillea* × *lewisii* 'King Edward' (yarrow)
15. *Schizostylis coccinea* 'Mrs Hegarty' (Kaffir lily)
16. *Campanula persicifolia* 'Telham Beauty'
17. *Campanula carpatica* var. *turbinata* 'Snowsprite'
18. *Iris pallida* 'Argentea Variegata'
19. *Stachys byzantina* 'Sheila McQueen' (lamb's tongue)
20. *Delphinium* × *belladonna* 'Wendy'
21. *Syringa microphylla* 'Superba' (lilac)
22. *Artemisia stelleriana* 'Nana'
23. *Aquilegia vulgaris* 'Nora Barlow' (columbine)
24. *Allium schoenoprasum*
25. *Sedum spurium* 'Atropurpureum'
26. *Centranthus ruber* (red valerian)
27. *Cynara cardunculus* Scolymus Group (globe artichoke)
28. *Salvia pratensis* Haematodes Group 'Indigo'
29. *Linum narbonense* 'Heavenly Blue'
30. *Geranium cinereum* 'Ballerina'
31. *Lavatera* 'Burgundy Wine' (tree mallow)

DESIGN FOR A BORDER IN HOT COLOURS

This mixed bed is the same size as the cool border, but is quite different in character; the colours are hot with brown-reds as the base tint, and the planting is carried out in overlapping triangular blocks. Like the other herbaceous bed, plant in groups, preferably of odd numbers, such as three, five, seven and so forth, to avoid a fussy and ineffective result.

As in the other plan, there are a few shrubs. A hebe and a purple-leaved viburnum create mass. There are also some very strong shapes, like the phormium, macleaya and phlomis. Repetitive vertical rhythms are created with lupins, eremurus and lobelia. Lower down, irises and day lilies echo

Hot colours are provided by late summer associations of Rudbeckia *'Herbstsonne' (syn. 'Autumn Sun') with* Helenium *'Coppelia' and golden solidago. The white* Phlox paniculata *'Fujiyama' is a cooling contrast.*

these forms. Flower contrast is provided by fennel, lupins and anthemis.

The colour scheme is rich with Venetian reds, set off by brown and purple foliage as in the heuchera, fennel and *Euphorbia dulcis* 'Chameleon'. *Pilosella aurantiaca*, kniphofia, helenium, lobelia, phlox and *Euphorbia griffithii* 'Fireglow' add brilliance. Yellow hemerocallis,

centaurea and golden grass punctuate the scheme. White flowers have a restful effect.

In both schemes, spring colour can be provided with bulbs and, as their leaves become unsightly, the herbaceous perennials soon mask them. As the years pass some herbaceous plants outgrow their space. These will need dividing and the healthier, younger sections replanted. No border will ever look exactly the same from year to year.

Key to plants

1. *Epimedium × rubrum* (barrenwort)
2. *Phlox paniculata*
3. *Heuchera* 'Red Spangles'
4. *Foeniculum vulgare* 'Giant Bronze' (bronze fennel)
5. *Phormium* 'Dark Delight'
6. *Lupinus* 'Noble Maiden'
7. *Aquilegia canadenis* (columbine)
8. *Hemerocallis* 'Whichford' (day lily)
9. *Heuchera americana*
10. *Echinacea purpurea* 'White Lustre' (purple cone flower)
11. *Macleaya cordata* 'Flamingo'
12. *Geum* 'Coppertone'
13. *Anthemis tinctoria* 'E.C. Buxton'
14. *Euphoria dulcis* 'Chameleon' (spurge)
15. *Phlomis russeliana*
16. *Heuchera micrantha* 'Palace Purple'
17. *Iris* 'Green Spot'
18. *Centaurea ruthenica* (knapweed)
19. *Eremurus × isabellinus* 'Pinokkio' (foxtail lily)
20. *Pilosella aurantiaca* (syn. *Hieracium aurantiacum*; hawkweed)
21. *Viburnum sargentii* 'Onondaga'
22. *Geranium sylvaticum* 'Album'
23. *Milium effusum* 'Aureum'
24. *Euphorbia griffithii* 'Fireglow' (spurge)
25. *Lobelia* 'Dark Crusader'
26. *Coreopsis verticillata* 'Moonbeam' (tickseed)
27. *Kniphofia galpinii* (red-hot poker)
28. *Lilium* 'Sterling Star'
29. *Hemerocallis* 'Stella de Oro' (day lily)
30. *Helenium* 'Kupfersprudel' (syn. 'Copper Spray') (sneezeweed)
31. *Hebe brachysiphon*

7 · INSTANT GARDENS

Lilium 'Mona Lisa' has striking flowers and is well suited to growing in a container for summer effect.

Starting from scratch, with no perennials at all, it is perfectly possible to create a truly instant garden in a few months. You could even buy ready-prepared plants from the nurseryman. These are often genetically programmed for fast growth and may be bedded out as plantlets.

One way to do this is to provide weed-free cultivated soil for a show of spring bulbs that are then followed by annuals or half-hardy plants. Alternatively, a succession of plants may be grown in mobile containers, which are brought out when the plants are in full flower and taken indoors again when they are over.

Bedding plants from seed

If you decide to opt for seeds, a much greater selection is open to you. Some early flowers may be planted out of doors. Biennials like wallflowers and forget-me-nots distribute their own seeds the summer before their early season flowering. You could, instead, raise them under glass and plant out the seedlings carefully in late spring. Hardy annuals may be sown into trays or pots in the autumn or spring immediately preceding and then planted out in late spring, after the frosts are over.

Seeds are sometimes packaged in vacuum-sealed foil sachets, enabling them to be viable for longer. Some are available coated in a fungicide. You will also be able to read on the packet if the seeds are F1 Hybrids. If so, they will be particularly vigorous and uniform. But not all plants are available as F1 Hybrids, so do not let this put you off choosing your favourites from the many reputable seed firms. Germination temperatures vary according to the plant, so follow the instructions on the packet.

When should you buy and plant? The selection available in ready-started juniors from the garden

Opposite: *Mixed pelargoniums, trailing lobelia, argyranthemums, nicotiana and grey-leaved helichrysum provide colourful, lush planting in terracotta containers.*

Always attractive and summery, nasturtiums weave their way into marigolds.

occur and become the essence of its appeal. In the same way, the interweaving patterns of related colours in a planned carpet of bedded plants could include some unexpected ones, say yellow ochre among a bed of pale or mid-blues with lilacs and purples. The colours of many bedding plants are vivid, in some cases to the point of being garish, so thoughtful planning is important.

Hot colour schemes Carpets of colour may be selected for closeness in the spectrum. So blood red would link with orange and chrome yellow. Truly hot effects are achieved by massing flame-coloured dwarf nasturtiums, mediated by their rounded blue-green leaves. Grow them in poor infertile soil, however, or the leaves will take over at the expense of the flowers. The cockscombs (*Celosia*), with their fluffed flowers, are just under 60cm (24in) tall and require really hot conditions. In midsummer they add fearful fiery reds and oranges. This is implied by the origin of its name *kelos*, Greek for flame. Similar heated colour schemes may be supported by some of the nemesias such as *N. strumosa* Carnival Series. They are mostly from South Africa but will do better in milder summers than the celosias. The vividly marked gazanias and the allied *Tithonia rotundifolia* (Mexican sunflower), however, will maintain the blazing bed. The gazanias are smaller, being under 38cm (15in), whereas the Mexican tithonias can vary from 80cm (18in) to 1.8m (6ft). Both have daisy flowers, which reminds me not to exclude the loved and familiar pot marigold, *Calendula officinalis*. For a warm yellow, ringed with white, the poached egg plant, *Limnanthes douglasii*, is a good and popular masser. It may be sown where it is to flower, and is only 15cm (6in) high, but the flowers last for months, ending in late summer.

centre will be more limited than if you choose your own seeds. On the other hand, work has been done on your behalf, and all you have to do is replant and then wait an average of only eight weeks, before the first flowers appear.

Colour in bedding

It is easy to create rich carpet patterns with geometric accuracy. You may decide to lay them in a strictly formal way or you could be more adventurous and design rich patterns on the lines of a handmade Persian carpet. I say handmade advisedly, because in such beautiful rugs, inaccuracies

Cool colour schemes Charming colour effects may be acquired using the blue-based reds and red-based purples we see in petunias, which are purple, magenta, cerise and pink. Rich blues and pastel mauves are also seen in the summer forget-me-nots, in *Anchusa capensis* and in the violet *Salvia splendens* Cleopatra Series or *S. farinacea* 'Victoria'. Cool hues like those of *Scabiosa atropurpurea* dwarf double mixed, which grow to about 45cm (1ft 6in), and the long-flowering *Phlox drummondii* may be added, with similarly coloured low-growing lobelias, *L. erinus,* and dwarf *Echium* 'Mixed Bedder' at foot. Flavour with one of the ageratums, such as *Ageratum houstonianum* 'Blue Danube', a lavender-coloured plant with a furred texture, growing to 45cm (1ft 6in).

Silver foliage Silver foliage is effective in mediating with both strong colours or pastels. It is traditional to add *Senecio cineraria* (dusty miller) or the more filigreed *S. cineraria* 'Silver Dew' as a calming influence with both cool and hot schemes. The perennial *Tanacetum ptarmiciflorum* (syn. *Pyrethrum ptarmicaeflorum*), known as silver feather, is often grown as an annual in this way. Silvery plants like these make good edges. They may also be massed in drifts or used as backing plants within colour schemes, where green would usually be the background colour. Young plants of *Helichrysum petiolare* are widely available for bedding out.

Formal planting schemes A formal geometric scheme could be achieved by a framework of edging plants, massed areas of colour and perhaps the odd focal point of a tall specimen plant, such as *Ricinus communis,* the castor oil plant. This is a tropical perennial reaching over 1.5m (5ft) and is often seen standing alone above a sea of colour.

Geometric schemes can certainly be efficient, and neat linear divisions of blocks of colour can be achieved quite simply with bedding. However,

The unfortunately named poached egg plant, Limnanthes douglasii, *is an invaluable summer plant because it lasts so well.*

straight lines between, say, a planting of begonias and blue ageratums is not a tranquil notion, and boundaries determined by box hedging or lawn and path edging make the enforced linear changes of colour logically acceptable.

If the site is clearly bounded and the planting areas are split into small units edged with brick, tiles or timber, a geometrical 'parterre' pattern with a carpet planting of fairground vitality could work well. You could mix the colours: reds with yellows, blues with oranges, purples with greens. The colours of the 25cm (10in) Californian poppy,

This red pelargonium is particularly beautiful backed by the perennial monarda.

Eschscholzia californica, provide superb satin yellows, oranges and reds amid light green foliage. A little smaller, the much-admired Livingstone daisy, *Mesembryanthemum criniflorum*, is another that carries a rainbow of colour, excluding blue. Both thrive in well-drained sunny sites.

These could be herded into geometric shapes. Structure may be added with clipped or topiaried box, and the plants within may be mixed with others. Alternatively, you may prefer to stick to one type and grade the colour. For example, the small French marigolds, *Tagetes patula*, come in several shades of gold, rust-red and orange.

Informal planting schemes In nature plants are distributed more randomly. Truly successful seed dispersal may well produce blocks of colour, but never with sharply defined edges. Massed shapes meander amoeba-like into other areas and, occasionally, individuals spread just that bit further, creating a new small colony in a foreign sea. This type of 'natural' random planting pattern can be very effective.

A few decades ago, traditional layouts involved curves drawn by hand on bare earth using trails of sand. I suggest that these curves should be generous sweeps, not tight and fussy, with dense masses interlinking and overlapping as drifts of colour weave in and out of one another in sensuous curves like abstract paintings. If the land is not level, emphasize the contours by following them with these sinuous curves. Planting drifts outlined in the previous chapter show some alternatives.

Infilling with annuals for sunny sites

The midsummer glories of herbaceous plants will have left room for massed swathes of spring colour in the form of naturalized bulbs. There will also be gaps in the summer border into which young container-grown plants, such as *Nicotiana alata* (syn. *N. affinis*) 'Grandiflora' (tobacco plants), can be transplanted. Tobacco plants, like many 'annual' plants, are really perennials, but they are often grown as annuals in cold countries. They are charming with plants such as lupins, delphiniums and eryngiums.

Also useful for repairing gaps in the planting scheme are the sun-loving osteospermums, often known as African daisies or Cape marigolds. (These plants used to be classified as *Dimorphotheca*.) There are many named cultivars to choose from as well as the species *O. jucundum* (syn. *O. barberae* and *Dimorphotheca barberae*). All grow to around 30cm (12in) tall, and in full sun the flowers last all summer long. They mix especially well with silver foliage such as that of the perennial *Stachys byzantina* (lamb's tongue) or the annual *Senecio cineraria* (dusty miller).

Blue flowers mix with more or less everything. *Linum narbonense*, the pale blue flax, is 50cm (20in) high and usually grown as an annual. Like love-in-a-mist and the tiny 15cm (6in) high nemophila, it may be sown where it is to flower.

Other useful infilling annuals are the mallows, *Lavatera trimestris,* providing mounds 80cm (2ft 6in) high of large-petalled white and pink flowers.

Pastels are refreshing in summer brilliance. Here white and lime green nicotianas work well with the flowers of Ruta graveolens *(common rue) and white eupatorium.*

Right: *Old-fashioned*
Dianthus barbatus *(sweet*
william) are always
welcome as they have so
many shades, from deep
velvet red, through pink,
to pure white. The holly-
hock behind is an ideal
companion.

Below: *The easily grown*
annual Nigella damas-
cena *(love-in-a-mist)*
provides a hazy sea of pale
blue and green as a foil for
alliums and irises.

Another cottage garden favourite, the scented sweet william, *Dianthus barbatus*, averages 45cm (18in) high and produces densely packed flower heads in pastel pinks, maroons and bi-colours. They flower early, taking over from the spring flowers.

By late summer *Cosmos bipinnatus* grow easily to 1m (3ft) tall, with single daisy flowers in the same colour range as the sweet williams, and fine light green foliage. The perennial chocolate cosmos, *Cosmos atrosanguineus*, often treated as annual as it will not overwinter unless thoroughly protected, has an irresistibly real scent of chocolate, but it is the rich dark velvet Venetian red of its petals that creates the demand for this bloom.

A combination of this with *Eucomis comosa* (syn. *E. punctata*), a late-flowering bulb with cream flower spikes of nearly the same height as the cosmos, and the small, rounded lemon flowers of *Scabiosa columbaria* var. *ochroleuca*, would make an unexpected but attractive marriage.

Lilies in pots and groups of marguerites may also be added as fillers. The latter prettily branched white daisy bushes are always a summery sight and fit in with every style of gardening. Both may be left in their pots, which will be hidden by the foliage of the perennials.

Infilling with instant plants is a real convenience, but do remember those vividly coloured pot plants from exotic places will rarely look right among temperate perennials. Neither hyacinth bulbs nor exotic gladiolus hybrids, for example, work well as mixers, although the modestly coloured species bluebell, *Hyacinthoides non-scripta* (syn. *Scilla nutans*), and the wild gladiolus, *G. communis* ssp. *byzantinus*, from the limestone of the Dinaric Alps, both integrate well.

Infilling for shady sites

I have been writing about plants for sunshine, but it would be a very unusual garden if there were no shade. For a softly natural drift in semi-shade the early flowers of honesty, *Lunaria annua*, either

Left: *This formal vase is planted with white marguerites and dwarf lime green nicotiana. At the foot is a blue hosta.*

Below: *Lunaria annua var.* variegata *(variegated white honesty) seeds itself, spreading freely in light shade.*

purple or white, are always effective. The flowers are followed by the familiar papery seedheads. The bedding plant leader for this has to be busy lizzie, *Impatiens* Novette or Duet Series. These Asian natives will grow successfully in shade and are marvellous for filling gaps. Bear in mind that slugs will like them even more than you do, so you may have to zap them in one way or another.

Giants

Besides offering rip-roaring colour, the short-lived plants include some large and exotic specimens. Pure white angel's trumpet, *Datura metel*, the stylish *Nicotiana sylvestris* or *Lilium candidum*, the Madonna lily, are exquisite examples.

My great favourites are less exotic, being annual hollyhocks, *Alcea rosea*, and by these I mean the old-fashioned, single types. I cannot do with the doubles, although I know that many people do like them very much. There are very pale yellows, crimsons, pinks and whites, and a very dark one, described as black but actually deep maroon, named *Alcea rosea* 'Nigra'. These giants may grow to over 1.8m (6ft), but they do suffer from rust, although this can be tackled by spraying. Hollyhocks are a traditional part of informal cottage garden style, but they do not need to be restricted to this. If the colours are carefully chosen, these architecturally formed plants can be deployed in more sophisticated designs.

For architectural drama, the white and whiskered *Cleome hassleriana* (syn. *C. spinosa*) 'Alba' is stylish, although the pink cleome is more usually seen. It bushes into a 1.2m (4ft) high plant by midsummer, and they are as remarkable a sight when grouped as they are when used as individuals. A real giant, the intense yellow sunflower, *Helianthus annuus* 'Russian Giant', is, of course, very familiar and much loved by youngsters. It quickly towers to nearly 3m (9ft) even when grown from seed. Summer supremacy is also seen in the powerful biennial mullein, *Verbascum*

bombyciferum, which, even in its first year, provides the garden with silvery soft, woolly leaves growing rosette-like from the hot, dry ground. During the second year it reaches its full form and is topped with yellow flowers. The contrastingly branched and spiked *Onopordum acanthium,* another silver-grey biennial, reaches 1.8m (6ft).

Climbers

I must not omit the beauties of instant climbers grown from seed. Some grow well in their own company, like the sweet pea, *Lathyrus odoratus*, with its effective tonal range of pastels to deep purple-reds. The old-fashioned *grandiflora* varieties

This form of wine-red Lathyrus odoratus *has a velvet texture which intensifies the colour.*

are remarkably fragrant, and the Spencer Hybrids particularly floriferous. If you do not want to grow them up an ugly green net, try growing some in a mass of branching twigs tied as a narrow wigwam, or over some shrubs, like the fastigiate rosemary.

The fast climber *Convolvulus tricolor* (syn. *Ipomoea rubrocaerulea*) 'Heavenly Blue', better known by its common name of morning glory, has the perfect convolvulus form but with enchanting blue flowers. The moon flower, *Ipomoea alba* (syn. *I. bona-nox* and *Calonyction aculeatum*), has equally fetching white flowers, which are fragrant as well. Both may be grown on a trellis or up evergreen shrubs to brighten the dense, dark foliage.

Cobaea scandens (cup-and-saucer vine) is really a Mexican perennial but, being very tender, is often treated as an annual. It grows thickly and rapidly in the summer season, producing dark green foliage and, if given an early indoor start, will soon be covered with flowers that resemble large Canterbury bells or the trumpet part of the daffodil. Through summer they develop from a luminous pale green to an intense purple, and they are invaluable for hasty repair where a permanent shrub or climber may have perished.

Two widely differing yellow climbers are worth noting. *Thunbergia alata* 'Susie' is an annual that has apricot yellow flowers with dense black eyes, which give rise to its common name, black-eyed Susan. Plant the seed in warmth in winter and do not transfer the young plants outside until the beginning of midsummer, five months later. The cooler toned acid yellow of *Tropaeolum peregrinum* (syn. *T. canariense*; canary creeper) will grow to the same height – about 3m (10ft) – as the thunbergia, but it has softer green, prettily divided leaves, which wrap themselves, firmly gripping a host shrub, such as a ceanothus.

Other annual nasturtiums, *Tropaeolum majus*, grown from seed may also climb a considerable height, but to gain flower rather than leaf, be cruel and grow them in poor, starved soil. The wonderful flame creeper *Tropaeolum speciosum* is a 'now you see

it, now you don't' plant. It grows from a rhizome and has vivid scarlet flowers, blue fruits and very pretty lobed, blue-green leaves. It is happiest on acid soils and will festoon dense columnar conifers to a considerable height in a season. However, it travels underground, and you may well find that although you thought it was dead, in reality it has ventured to another site where it will start again.

Containers

Containers are also important when considering 'instant' effects. In some gardens there may be no planting beds – town yards are often without soil, for example. Some inhospitable climates make it nearly impossible to grow permanent plants. Such conditions call for planters, which can be cared for indoors and brought out when conditions permit.

Cooling white is the theme for these summer containers. Pelargoniums, osteospermums and nicotianas fulfil the requirement.

For readers who live in extremely warm climates, the instant summer garden may include exotics like *Strelitzia reginae* (bird-of-paradise flower), *Turnera ulmifolia* (Cuban buttercup), *Phoenix roebelenii* (miniature or pygmy date palm) or the elegant *Clivia caulescens*, together with, perhaps, a group of succulents.

Containers and composts Most containers need to be moved into view when they are at their best and retired for recuperation, so they must be light enough to move or be on wheels. Those that are permanently out-of-doors, like large troughs, must be frost-proof and planted up *in situ*. The larger the pot the less you will have to water, but all containers

Warm-coloured terracotta is an ideal container for summer annuals, which include felicia, phlox, verbenas, petunias and alstroemeria.

should be raised above ground level for easy drainage. Drainage holes must be covered with broken crocks followed by a layer of coarse grit. Above this, a layer of peat may be added to help to conserve water. Alternatively, polymer crystals which swell and hold water may be incorporated into the compost. These are available from garden centres. Complete the planting by adding a proprietary compost, filling to about 2.5cm (1in) of the top.

Plants for containers Summer annuals are invaluable for planters. Petunias and pelargoniums, frequently supported by *Helichrysum petiolare,* lead the field, followed by trailing lobelias and verbenas. However, consider the fragrant heliotrope, glamorous begonias, campanulas, gazanias and lilies.

The range of half-hardy fuchsias is a blessing in container gardens. The trailing flowers last all summer, and they may be used in combination with trailing white *Campanula isophylla,* lobelias, verbena and ivies.

Pelargoniums (often misnamed geraniums) are, like fuchsias, half-hardy perennials. There are four main kinds. Zonal pelargoniums have highly decorative marked foliage; Regal ones are more compact, with lush flowers; Ivy-leaved pelargoniums are wonderful in containers because they trail; and finally there are the scented-leaved, tiny species pelargoniums for smaller pots. The flowers continue as long as you dead-head the plant. Like fuchsias, they combine well with trailing white, pink or purple verbena, blue and powder blue lobelia, trailing small-leaved ivies and other annuals.

Marguerites and osteospermums produce daisy flowers for containers throughout the summer months. The silver and lime green foliage of *Helichrysum petiolare* blends with every scheme.

Most plants will cope with containers, given the right size of pot, compost and feeding. The amount of watering will depend on the plants as well as on where you site them. In light shade, impatiens, some violas, lobelia, erinus, *Heuchera × brizoides* and, of course, ferns and ivies will do well.

Left: *Hanging baskets are overflowing with mixed pelargoniums, lobelias, helichrysums and fuchsias.*

Below: *This hanging basket contains trailing fuchsias, nasturtiums and petunias.*

DESIGN FOR A SUMMER SEASON

This semicircular bed is planted for summer only. The radius of the outer ring is 5m (16ft) and the border is 2m (6ft) deep. This provides generous room for a good display. Plant ready-grown seedlings or put seeds and bulbs where they are to flower. Always keep back some plants in pots to fill in later, in case the summer is dry and there are failures. Grow late-flowering asters in containers to replace any fading flowers. Prepare the bed during the previous year by digging over, removing weeds and working in either rotted manure or compost. If the soil is heavy, leave it rough through winter so that the rain and frost can break it down. In spring create a fine tilth ready for sowing or transplanting any young seedlings.

Annuals require careful planning and this is easily done on paper, if you carefully note height, colour and period of flower.

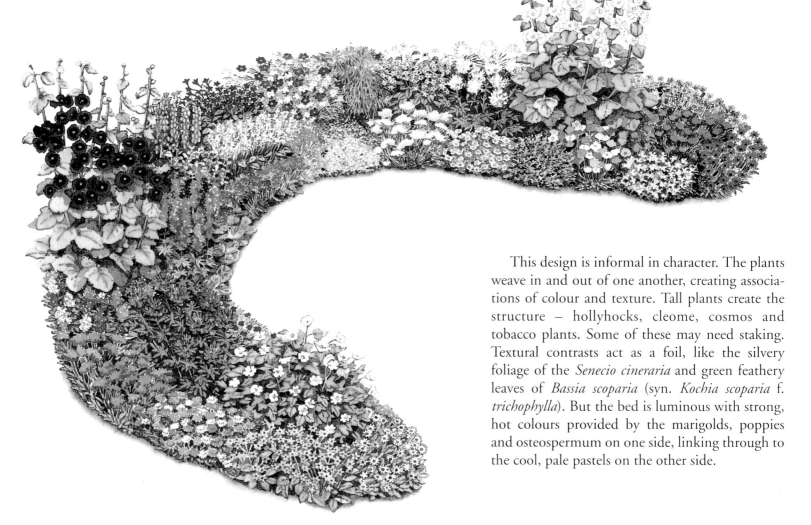

This design is informal in character. The plants weave in and out of one another, creating associations of colour and texture. Tall plants create the structure – hollyhocks, cleome, cosmos and tobacco plants. Some of these may need staking. Textural contrasts act as a foil, like the silvery foliage of the *Senecio cineraria* and green feathery leaves of *Bassia scoparia* (syn. *Kochia scoparia* f. *trichophylla*). But the bed is luminous with strong, hot colours provided by the marigolds, poppies and osteospermum on one side, linking through to the cool, pale pastels on the other side.

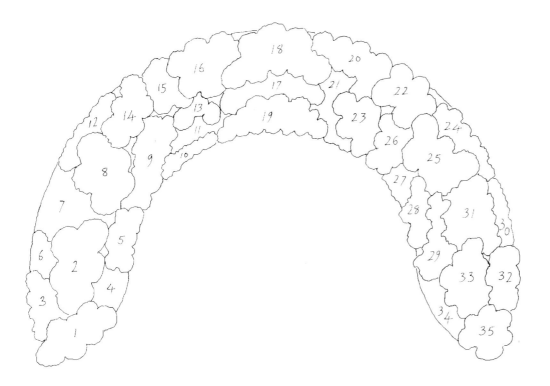

Key to plants

1. *Osteospermum* 'Whirligig'
2. *Lavatera trimestris* (annual mallow)
3. *Nicotiana* 'Lime Green'
4. *Nemophila menziesii* (Californian bluebell)
5. *Dianthus chinensis* (Indian pink)
6. *Iberis umbellata* (candytuft)
7. *Limonium sinuatum* (blue and lavender hybrids)
8. *Cleome hassleriana* (syn. *C. spinosa*) 'Pink Queen' (spider flower)
9. *Consolida ajacis* (syn. *Delphinium consolida*; larkspur)
10. *Begonia* × *carrierei* (syn. *B. semperflorens*; bedding begonia)
11. *Lobelia erinus* 'Blue Heaven'
12. *Matthiola incana* (ten-week stock)
13. *Helichrysum petiolare*
14. *Alcea rosea* (syn. *Althaea rosea*) 'Nigra' (hollyhock)
15. *Moluccella laevis* (bells of Ireland)
16. *Nicotiana alata* (red hybrid; tobacco plant)
17. *Salvia sclarea* var. *turkestanica* (clary)
18. *Cosmos bipinnatus*
19. *Cynoglossum amabile* 'Firmament'
20. *Bassia scoparia* (syn. *Kochia scoparia* f. *trichophylla*; burning bush)

21. *Anchusa capensis* 'Blue Bird' (Chinese forget-me-not)
22. *Nicotiana alata* (white, cream and green hybrids; tobacco plant)
23. *Gypsophila elegans* 'Covent Garden' (baby's breath)
24. *Salvia splendens* Carabiniere Series
25. *Cleome hassleriana* (syn. *C. spinosa*) 'Helen Campbell' (spider flower)
26. *Limonium sinuatum* (white and yellow hybrids)
27. *Limnanthes douglasii* (poached egg plant)
28. *Senecio cineraria* (dusty miller)
29. *Papaver nudicaule* (Iceland poppy)
30. *Tagetes* 'Paprika' (French marigold)
31. *Alcea rosea* (syn. *Althaea rosea*; hollyhock)
32. *Rudbeckia hirta* 'Burpeeii'
33. *Eschscholzia californica* (Californian poppy)
34. *Tagetes* 'Lemon Gem' (French marigold)
35. *Osteospermum* 'Gaiety'

8 · ORNAMENTAL GRASSES

In a grass border in high summer the oat-like flowers of Stipa gigantea *(golden oats) provide a parchment-coloured haze above the greenery.*

The subtleties of grass, so appreciated in childhood, are often forgotten when we become adult and serious. What a loss this is, for there are many delicate shapes and patterns. Some are tall, reedy and slim, others are stiff spikes or small velvety mounds of fine grasses. They may react to every breeze, swaying and rustling. The flowers may be mere puffs of fluff, silvered floating hairs, suspended panicles or furry tufts. The colours are soft shades of neutrals, here creamy, there tinged with pink, another parchment colour. In sunlight the flowers become luminous, insubstantial silhouettes, adding patterns, rhythms and textures to the garden in summer.

The subtleties of ornamental grasses were largely unrealized by gardeners until relatively recent. However, both William Robinson and Gertrude Jekyll used them within their border schemes, recognizing their intrinsic charm and their supreme compatibility with other plants. Today they are increasingly popular both as 'solo artistes' and as active members of the perennial chorus. They are seen to blend equally well with shrubs or with herbaceous plants. Whether they are 'real' grasses (Gramineae), or sedges or rushes, they have a place in mixed planting schemes.

Colour is not the first priority when using grasses. Look rather for strong linear patterns and the translucent shimmering flower heads. Some, like *Cortaderia selloana* (pampas grass) and *Arundo donax* (giant reed), are distinguished in their own right, having the architectural presence of garden trees, but most are exceedingly amenable to mixing in the herbaceous scheme of things.

Flowers and panicles

In flower beds where colour is carefully selected, the muted colours and shades of grasses can be used to prevent a planting scheme from becoming either overwhelming or bland.

Among yellow flowers, consider planting clumps of the striking pampas grass, *Cortaderia selloana* 'Gold Band'. This is 1.5m (5ft) tall by 90cm (36in) wide, and has tousled leaves and large white plumes, borne in late summer. Golden berberis or elder could also be used, as well as some of the golden herbaceous plants like verbascum and helenium. This would be an indigestible mix if there were not some softening blues like catmint or *Delphinium × belladonna* to add some contrast. The feather reed grass *Calamagrostis × acutiflora* 'Overdam' would also work well in this border. The 90cm (36in) mounds have arching white and green striped leaves and carry feathery flowers by late summer.

All the miscanthus make themselves welcome among other plants. The huge *M. sacchariflorus* reaches over 3m (9ft) each summer. It has tall canes supporting 'falls' of blue-grey leaves. Moist soil is a requirement, which means that it is a fine friend for the magnificent reddened rheums and browned rodgersias.

Even though they are slightly smaller *Miscanthus sinensis* cultivars will nevertheless require some space. Both the flowers and the foliage are attractive. A taller cultivar like *M. s.* 'Malepartus' reaches to more than 2m (6ft). Its broad leaves have a conspicuous silver spine and

Growing from a gravel mulch and thriving in sunny, well-drained soil is the grass Stipa tenuissima, *mixed with the silver-grey* Artemisia stelleriana, Tulbaghia violacea, *green-flowering* Nicotiana langsdorffii *and* Sedum spurium *'Atropurpureum'.*

the captivating flower plumes are a silky mahogany red in summer, which combines very successfully with tawny and dusty pink chrysanthemums.

Chinese silver grass, *M. s.* 'Silberfeder'(syn. 'Silver Feather'), is probably the most admired. Growing over 2m (6ft) high, it is quite large enough to contend with the shrubby *Eupatorium ligustrinum* with its dusky carmine-rose flowers. It has a tall, arching habit, with wide ribbon leaves and a late summer show of silvery pinkish-white plumes. *M. s.* 'Silberfeder' requires space to display its true beauty. The exceptionally elegant *M. s.* 'Gracillimus' is another favourite, at 1.5m (5ft). Its foliage is more finely textured than the type species, curling rather than arching. Inflorescences carry this decoration further, with an elaborately curled form, rather Art Nouveau in its manner.

The porcupine-striped *M. s.* 'Zebrinus' has transverse yellow stripes along the length of its 90cm (36in) leaves. This accommodating grass will grow in most situations, possibly backed by the yellow-rayed daisy flowers of the huge *Inula magnifica* or the bright yellow *Rudbeckia* 'Goldquelle'. A more subtle colour combination would be with the greeny white umble-flowered *Angelica archangelica*, another mighty plant. There is a danger that these tall plant groups may crowd out the miscanthus, so space must be allowed around it. Indeed, all these tall grasses need space to be seen at their best.

Some of the more modest low-growing grasses would be fetching, like the mossy green mounds of *Festuca gautieri* (syn. *F. scoparia*) or the fine slim-foliaged *Melica altissima* 'Atropurpurea'. Or consider clumps of *Sesleria autumnalis*, a green grass only 45cm (18in) high, with cream panicles spikes in autumn, and include a mass of the small *Deschampsia flexuosa* 'Tatra Gold', which has needle-fine blades and bronze flowers in midsummer. The species *D. flexuosa*, which is only 45cm (18in), also does well in shade. I have a fondness for the 1.2m (4ft) high *Deschampsia caespitosa* 'Goldschleier' (syn. 'Golden Veil'),

known also as tufted hair grass. It flowers in midsummer with a haze of tiny silver-green flowers ageing to gold as summer progresses. Try this captivating grass in the company of *Phlomis russeliana*, a plant with roughened leaves and yellow whorls of flowers up the stem.

The oat-like *Stipa gigantea* is another wonderful grass for the summer herbaceous bed. It makes a large clump, about 75cm (30in) wide at the base, and the massed clouds of glistening purple oat flowers are suspended high in the air to about 1.8m (6ft). With it, crinkled red and mauve annual poppies, or the pink perennial *Papaver orientale* 'Turkish Delight', is enchanting. Many of the smaller grasses have quite charismatic flower panicles. The pennisetums are tussocky grasses, usually under 60cm (24in) tall and, as the common name fountain grass would suggest, the shining narrow green leaves are covered in mid- to late-summer with softly curving, white flowers looking rather like fat furry caterpillars. *Pennisetum setaceum* 'Rubrum', known as crimson fountain grass, comes from Africa but is now widely used in garden design.

Among other grasses with attractive flowers, *Briza media,* the common quaking grass, is fun, with its trembling hanging lockets of flowers reaching 45cm (18in). And the foxtail barley, *Hordeum jubatum*, just short of 75cm (30in), has a brief month of beauty in early summer when the fanning silver-green barley flowers shimmer.

Colour in foliage

For colour in grasses, look to the leaves. Probably the boldest is *Imperata cylindrica* 'Red Baron'. This scarlet-coloured grass, known as Japanese blood grass, is a little over 30cm (12in) tall and can be grown as a spreading rhizomatous mass in light shade. Almost as strongly coloured are some of the sedges, such as the brown *Carex flagellifera* and *C. petriei*, both 30cm (12in) high. These plants appreciate retentive soil, so will be well suited

Opposite: Carex elata 'Aurea' (Bowles' golden sedge) merges with Hosta 'Buckshaw Blue', backed by Sambucus racemosa 'Sutherland Gold' (golden elder).

Milium effusum *'Aureum' distributes itself easily. Here it is doing well in the company of moisture-loving trollius and* Hosta fortunei *var.* albopicta.

beside some of the smaller blue or green hostas, or some of the brown-leaved astilbes. *C. oshimensis* 'Evergold' is invaluable for all-year-round garden use, and it will also cope with partial shade. Consequently, it is often used for edging. Less tidy in habit but attractively butter yellow, the hardy *Milium effusum* 'Aureum' spreads widely by seed, particularly in shaded sites. Another brilliantly yellow grass, *Carex elata* 'Aurea' is the well-known

Bowles' golden sedge, a great favourite of E.A. Bowles of Myddelton House. It needs damp soil and will grow to 60cm (24in). There is another most unusual sedge, *Carex* 'Frosted Curls', a glamorous plant with finely curled hair leaves growing to a height and spread of 30cm (12in).

Other yellow leaves are to be found in *Acorus gramineus* 'Ogon', an evergreen curving gold-green grass, which is about 15cm (6in) high and wide.

Hakonechloa macra 'Alboaurea', from Japan, is a positive yellow with fine green stripes. It gradually ages to a vivid rust-red, which cannot be ignored. It is small, 25cm (10in) high, and drapes itself over the ground.

Blue grasses are always popular. They grow pleasingly with the silver artemisias and the spiky blue-grey eryngiums in hot, dry conditions. The blue fescue, *Festuca glauca,* is the most frequently seen and is a neat 25cm (12in) high, but do also consider *Elymus magellanicus* (syn. *Agropyron magellanicum*), which has needle-fine 60cm (24in) tall grass spikes rigidly pointing skywards, like the erect stiff needle leaves of the 60cm (24in) blue oat grass, *Helictotrichon sempervirens*, although this grass is greatly softened by floating plumes overhead. The other famous blue-grey grass was Miss Jekyll's favourite, *Leymus arenarius* (syn. *Elymus arenarius*; lymegrass). Under 60cm (24in) tall, this rampantly adventurous grass is used effectively in sand dunes to tackle erosion. The coarse turquoise-blue blades are seductive, but if you do plant it, aim to restrict growth by keeping it in large containers beneath the soil so that it can grow to its full height.

Variegated grasses are also much admired in a border, but the most used one, *Phalaris arundinacea* var. *picta*, generally known as gardener's garters or ribbon grass, is another invasive specimen. The very beautiful *Glyceria maxima* var. *variegata* is a clotted cream colour with green, but it really must have very damp soil.

Grasses with grass-like plants

Successful design often depends on repeating rhythms. Grasses may be grown with yuccas for drama or they can be enhanced by phormiums, from the prima donna *P. tenax* down to the small *P.* 'Bronze Baby', whose sword-like leaves will emphasize the delicacy of the grasses. Other linear patterns could be made using irises and sisyrinchiums with grasses. Their flowers will add

Left: *Requiring moist ground,* Glyceria maxima *var.* variegata *has a cream rather than white variegation. It is a beautiful grass when allowed space to drift beside water.*

Below: Phalaris arundinacea *var.* picta *(gardener's garters) can be invasive. It is seen here growing alongside* Achillea *'Coronation Gold' with* Rosa *'Iceberg' behind.*

Drifts of Muscari botry-*oides and miniature daffodils mingle with orange-brown* Libertia peregrinans.

Opposite: Cortaderia selloana *(pampas grass) makes huge creamy panicles, which withstand wind. Here they can be seen beyond the massive heavy foliage of* Gunnera manicata.

spots of colour, and throughout the summer their sword-like leaves will merge with the grasses. Coloured foliage, such as that of the glowing rusty-orange *Libertia peregrinans*, adds distinction to grass-like shapes as it winds its way by stolons among other plants. Later in summer, agapanthus hybrids and *Schizostylis coccinea* (Kaffir lily) will do the same. Then the grasses begin to turn a beautiful end-of-year parchment. If left uncut, they will provide winter drama, standing indistinct in autumn mists or glistening with frost.

The giants

Finally, I should have a word about the giants. I mean the pampas grasses, the giant reed, *Arundo donax,* and, of course, some bamboos.

Some, as we have seen, will co-habit happily with their herbaceous equivalents, sure of their tall status. Others perform best as isolated specimens, providing vertical height and focal accent to the garden. The supreme pampas grasses, cultivars of *Cortderia selloana*, are splendid used in this way. There are some varieties worth noting. I have already described *C. s.* 'Gold Band' with its yellow foliage and 1.5m (5ft) height, but *C. s.* 'Monstrosa'

is a monument of immense cream plumes reaching 2.7m (9ft) by late summer. The smaller *C. s.* 'Pumila' is more compact at 1.2m (4ft) and so is a candidate for smaller spaces.

The rustling evergreen foliage makes bamboos good associates with summer grasses and useful all-year-round performers, but bamboos are to be treated with respect. Many are hardy and tough, but their colonizing power makes them a potential threat. When they are planted near water they make massive grassy clumps of canes, wonderful in reflection. The glossy foliage of *Phyllostachys bambusoides* is 3cm (1½in) wide and lush green. Many of the bamboos have coloured canes, like the purple-black *Phyllostachys nigra* 'Boryana' or the yellow-gold canes of the tender *Himalayacalamus hookerianus* (syn. *Arundinaria hookeriana*). The hardy *Phyllostachys violascens* has unusual striped culms (stems). But bamboos are mostly grown for their 4m (13ft) or over height, their clump-forming habit and attractive evergreen foliage. To restrain the spread you may consider digging a shallow trench around your specimen and haunching the sides. *Fargesia murieliaea* (syn. *Arundinaria murieliae*) is the least invasive, but the pretty golden striped foliage of *Pleioblastus auricomus* (syn. *P. viridistriatus*), although only 1.2m (4ft) high, is rampageous. Restraint is very necessary, and they can be difficult to remove, so do consider carefully before planting.

The choice of grasses is expanding as more interest is taken in them by gardeners, but do always check the needs of the plant before you buy, because growing conditions are particularly important with grasses. Some really must have damp sites and look wonderful with water, while others demand dry, hot sites. Be aware of the ultimate size and allow them space to achieve their full glory. And finally, remember that not all grasses make static clumps. Many will invade and destroy, and you will need to keep your observant eye on them. But as part of summer's natural bounty they are, I think, indispensable.

DESIGN FOR A GRASS GARDEN

Grasses, sedges and bamboos evoke an image of wild beauty and last through summer. Here, a windbreak is provided by bamboos and tall grasses, plus the dark foliage of purple-leaved elder and the bronze leaves of rodgersia. The area measures 9–10m (30–32ft) by 8–9m (26–30ft). In this sunny garden there is a pool and some areas are permanently wet. These are planted with

grasses, irises and hostas. In other parts of the garden, different grasses and perennials work well together in drier soil conditions. These need a free-draining, sand-based soil with added humus.

Ornamental grasses are easy to grow compared with many perennial plants. Some are compact; others are tall and swaying. Although most grasses prefer sun, they are adaptable to soil and temperature differences and do not have many disease problems.

Some, like phalaris, glyceria and *Pleioblastus pygmaeus* (syn. *Arundinaria pygmaea*), are invasive so will need reducing every other year, or surrounding with a barrier of submerged plastic or non-perishable edging approximately 30cm (1ft) or more deep. Alternatively, keep the grasses in large containers to restrict the roots.

Many grasses are attractive throughout autumn and in winter, when their parchment-coloured leaves lighten winter shadows, but it is always better to cut back the flowers before they become untidy. Irises, day lilies and crocosmia are planted for the grass-like effect of their leaves, which harmonize with grassy forms. These plants also add colourful flowers. Further summer colour and contrasting shapes are provided by rudbeckias and euphorbias.

Key to plants

1. *Fargesia murieliae* (syn. *Arundinaria murieliae*, *Thamnocalamus spathaceus*; muriel bamboo)
2. *Phalaris arundinacea* var. *picta* (gardener's garters, ribbon grass)
3. *Lobelia* 'Will Scarlet'
4. *Hosta sieboldiana*
5. *Miscanthus sinensis* 'Zebrinus' (zebra grass)
6. *Pennisetum orientale* (oriental fountain grass)
7. *Sedum* 'Herbstfreude' (*syn.* 'Autumn Joy')
8. *Armeria maritima* 'Alba' (thrift)
9. *Festuca gautieri* (syn. *F. scoparia*)
10. *Pennisetum alopecuroides* (Australian fountain grass)
11. *Miscanthus sinensis* 'Variegatus' (striped eulalia grass)
12. *Euphorbia griffithii* 'Fireglow' (spurge)
13. *Iris sibirica*
14. *Rudbeckia fulgida* var. *sullivantii* 'Goldsturm' (cone flower)
15. *Deschampsia caespitosa* (tufted hair grass)
16. *Miscanthus sinensis* (Chinese silver grass)
17. *Hemerocallis* 'Black Magic'
18. *Miscanthus sinensis* 'Gracillimus' (maiden grass)
19. *Crocosmia* 'Lucifer'
20. *Sambucus nigra* 'Purpurea' (elder)
21. *Miscanthus sacchariflorus* (amur silver grass, silver banner grass)
22. *Carex oshimensis* 'Evergold' (Japanese sedge grass)
23. *Hemerocallis* 'Golden Chimes'
24. *Arrhenatherum elatius* ssp. *bulbosum* 'Variegatum' (bulbous oat grass)
25. *Arundinaria pygmaea* (pygmy bamboo)
26. *Rodgersia aesculifolia* 'Irish Bronze'
27. *Astilbe chinensis*
28. *Iris pseudacorus* (flag)

9 · IN SUN AND IN SHADE

Opposite: A seat is built around a tree in woodland shade. In front are massed white Lilium regale and pink Geranium × oxonianum 'Wargrave Pink'.

The right plant in the right place is the natural order of things. Gardeners who observe this grow successful plants. Usually. But plants have proved to be amazingly adaptable and have moved around the globe – plants from New Zealand, Chile, China, the Cape and the Himalayas have emigrated as successfully as people.

Nevertheless, observing a plant's basic requirements is crucial, whether it be for acid soil, for high moisture content, or for protection when the temperature falls below 5°C (41°F) in winter, or for shade.

In a hot gravelled garden Allium aflatunense, Armeria maritima, eucomis and a dark red iris thrive in the sun.

Natural shade in the wild usually means growing beneath deciduous trees, which may create a dappled light in summer and provide a period of full light in winter and spring. Only some conifers allow no light whatsoever to penetrate, and in these conditions there will be hardly any ground cover at all.

Normally, where there is soil there will be a plant to suit. Even in the infertile sand of hot deserts, after a rare hour or two of rain, 'the desert blooms', and in cold stone deserts some toughies manage to gain a foothold. So the inclination of the plant world seems to be 'hang in there', adapt and survive.

Your own small habitat is certain to support some plants, whether you tend it or not. But what is the best characteristic of the garden? Is it warm, sunny and protected? Do you have a naturally shaded area? Is the soil reasonably moisture retentive? A positive look at the assets will mean a positive selection of plants.

Hot, dry sites

Converting deserts with camel dung has proved effective in areas of the Middle East. In your own scale of things you can incorporate rotted fibrous manure into exposed, dry soil. This will lighten and aerate it and also help to conserve moisture and nutrients. But the key to success is the emphatic word, mulch. Conserving water is necessary, even for plants that require free-draining ground. Mulching the surface with pulverized bark is one possibility, but in very hot, arid conditions fine gravel, laid about 2.5cm (1in) thick, will help to prevent surface evaporation as well as restrict weed growth and, to some extent, keep the soil a little cooler.

Agaves must be in warm sunny places if they are to thrive. This one, A. americana *'Marginata', is sited with other sun-loving plants, such as verbena and the grey-leaved* Anthemis cretica, *which has cool white flowers.*

Structure plants and their associates for hot, dry sites As always, it is easier to plan by establishing the structure plants first. These include the deciduous or evergreen shrubs and the prima donna plants – the eye-catchers.

In the summer some of the berberis family and escallonias can be used to add small-leaved evergreen backing, and escallonias will flower in midsummer. The apple-blossom pink *Escallonia* 'Slieve Donard' and the small 90cm (36in) *E.* 'Red Elf' are truly evergreen, and these could be sited near *Olearia* × *macrodonta* (New Zealand holly), whose sage green foliage is also evergreen but has a

quite different texture from the glossy leaves of the escallonias. The olearia's panicles of white daisy flowers are very pretty in midsummer, and they associate particularly well in sunshine with the white crinkled flowers of *Papaver orientale* 'Perry's White'.

Associates that have a scratchy approach to life could provide a cool scheme for a hot site. The 1m (3ft) tall globe thistle, *Echinops ritro*, with blue spiked spheres for flowers, and the statuesque, 1.2m (4ft) tall, *Acanthus spinosus* would make a characterful group. But add some softening effects, like the velvet-leaved evergreen rock rose *Cistus*

'Peggy Sammons', a 75cm (30in) high shrub with a mass of pale pink flowers.

Add touches of restrained colour with a purple sage, *Salvia officinalis* Purpurascens Group, *Hebe* 'Mrs E. Tennant', a fairly hardy shrub, growing to about 90cm (36in), with violet flower panicles, plus the intensely blue spikes of *Salvia × superba* 'Superba'. Then perhaps you might like to include the very low-growing *Helianthemum* 'Rhodanthe Carneum' (syn. 'Wisley Pink').

The supremely aristocratic foliage of *Melianthus major* (honey bush) makes this a glamorous subject for sunny, dry and gravelled gardens. The stems, with their sage green leaves, can reach 2–3m (6–9m), so allow plenty of space. It is not frost-hardy but looks wonderful with Old Shrub roses. Alternatively, when seen growing from a gravel mulch in dry conditions, it blends particularly well with the 90cm (36in) *Centaurea ruthenica*, which has canary yellow, fluffed flowers on tall branching stems, above dark green rather fern-like foliage.

Smaller plants to work in with this group of dictators could be *Anthemis* 'Tetworth', a white, daisy-flowered, 60cm (24in) high shrub with finely cut silver leaves, and *Coreopsis verticillata* 'Moonbeam'. The mid-green foliage of the coreopsis would help to soften the group.

In these hot, dry areas there are other dramatic shapes that could be used. *Yucca filamentosa* or *Euphorbia characias* could be grown with low mounds of the evergreen but not completely hardy *Ceanothus* 'Italian Skies' (Californian lilac), with its Oxford blue flowers. The 1.5m (5ft) tall *Romneya coulteri*, the Californian tree poppy, would provide a wonderful contrast, with its large incised grey foliage and succession of crinkled white poppies with yellow stamens.

Emphasize the yellows by selecting *Yucca recurvifolia* 'Marginata' for its compact gold-edged leaves and in quiet anticipation of its late creamy flower panicles. Add some *Milium effusum* 'Aureum' for a softening effect.

Colour in dry sunny gardens Many of the grey-leaved plants are equipped to cope with hot sun. The most commonly used are *Convolvulus cneorum, Stachys byzantina, Helichrysum italicum* (syn. *H. angustifolium*), *Senecio cineraria* 'White Diamond' and most artemisias and phormiums. The neat, small, grass clumps of *Festuca glauca, Leymus arenarius* (syn. *Elymus arenarius*) and *Helictotrichon sempervirens* are quite blue in colour and will also thrive in hot, dry situations. Many eryngiums would echo the blue, like *Eryngium bourgatii, E. variifolium* and the paler *E. maritimum*.

Yellows and lime greens work well together in the sun. Euphorbia characias ssp. wulfenii *provides a dramatic structure, which is softened by the far smaller* E. polychroma *and* Argyranthemum *'Jamaica Primrose'.*

If the yellow-leaved tree lupin, *Lupinus arboreus*, were to be the dominant form in a summer grouping, lemon-yellowed flowered shrubs such as *Potentilla fruticosa* 'Primrose Beauty', the small *Helianthemum* 'Wisley Primrose' and the cooler yellow achilleas would reflect the same lemony hues. There are warmer yellows for these conditions, like the flowers of *Halimium* 'Susan'. The evening primroses (*Oenothera*) provide bright sunshine yellows, which distribute themselves rapidly by seed around the garden, but for very rich, bright colours the alstroemerias are the likely winners. The Peruvian lily comes from Chile, is 80cm (30in) tall and offers a wide range of yellows, through apricot pink to pure orange. But they really are very invasive and will surround and overcome other plants, so site them with care.

Although the flowers are over by early summer, the shade-loving Helleborus foetidus *Wester Flisk Group has attractive ground-covering foliage.*

Traditionally, pink is one of the favoured colour associations with greys. *Gypsophila* 'Rosy Veil' is a neat 30cm (12in) perennial, which is captivating with the silver velvet *Stachys byzantina*. Associating with it, the white form of the neat green foliage of *Parahebe catarractae*, a small, 15cm (6in) plant, and the similarly sized *Erodium glandulosum* (syn. *E. macradenum*), with its cool pink flowers, plus the woolly grey leaved mat of *Thymus doerleri* 'Bressingham Pink', nestling contentedly on the gravel mulch. Add substance to all this with a group of the tiny red-leaved *Berberis thunbergii* 'Bagatelle', plus a dwarf fuschia such as *F.* 'Tom Thumb' and red valerian, *Centranthus ruber* var. *atrococcineus*.

Shade in the garden

Paradoxically, shade in the summer garden may be one of its greatest assets. As a glade of sunlight is welcomed in a dark wood, so pools of shade are most appreciated in a sunny space. Too much of one without the other becomes monotonous. The glowing summer garden is all the more enticing if there are dark recesses.

If your garden space does not include these areas of shade, this can be achieved by planting trees that are noted either for their dense or for their light-filtering canopy. Alternatively, you may be able to focus upon the north-facing area of the garden and make more of it.

Structure in dense shade Many of the evergreens are stalwart shade-lovers. Some have intensely dark foliage, like *Prunus lusitanica* (Portuguese laurel), and others have glossy, light-reflective leaves, like the common or cherry laurel. If the soil is acidic, rhododendrons, skimmias, gaultheria and camellias will be happy. Otherwise, the sculptured forms of plants such as *Fatsia japonica* can add an architectural touch.

As for herbaceous perennials, there are some very attractive and enticing plants to enhance the shady summer depths. In my selection, I am assuming that the soil will be damp.

For really dense shades, with very litle light penetration, it is best to aim for green ground cover. Evergreens that serve all year round will provide green foundation shapes. *Ruscus aculeatus* (butcher's broom), which is usually only about 75cm (30in) high, is tough. Plant a few females with a male plant to ensure red autumn berries. Aucubas are other uncomplaining evergreens. Look for the glossy narrow foliage of *A. japonica* 'Salicifolia', the yellow variegation of *A. j.* 'Crotonifolia', and a prize form, *A. j.* 'Rozannie', which has large red fruits. Ground ivies are reliable, too, as are some fanning ferns like the *Dryopteris* varieties, which will add tall texture. Winter-flowering *Sarcococca humilis*, known also as sweet box of Christmas box, will survive, particularly on chalk.

Many of the herbaceous 'doers' for such situations are winter- or spring-flowering, like the Corsican hellebores, such as nettles *Lamium galeobdon* 'Variegatum' and the varieties of *Vinca major* (periwinkle). However, the leaves – some of them variegated – will often continue to provide good effects for dense shade in summer. Here, *Iris foetidissima* 'Variegata' (stinking iris) is particularly useful. Small *Vinca minor* 'Argenteovariegata' can pick up on this lighter theme, and lamiums too have variegations, such as *Lamium maculatum* 'Beacon Silver' or *L.m.* 'White Nancy'

Dappled shade Most shade, however, is dappled, and this opens the doors to a larger variety of plants, many of which will flower during the summer. Again I will assume that the soil is not very dry, although many ferns like adiantum, blechnum and athyrium, are adapatable for dry conditions as well. Those that are at home in light woodlands are useful: forms of *Polypodium vulgare* and *Blechnum spicant* (hard fern) do well and grow to between 10cm and 45cm (4–18in) high. The familiar wild fern *Dryopteris filix-mas*, the male

fern, has an elegant habit and is obliging as to its cultivation needs. It may reach 1.2m (4ft) in height. The next most easily grown is the lady fern, *Athyrium filix-femina*, which is of a similar height and habit.

You will find a vast choice of other fern varieties, from the glossy *Asplenium scolopendrium* (hart's tongue fern) to the tiny spleen-worts (*Asplenium*), which prefer a limey soil. The giant soloists, which do need space and damp soil or wet sites to show themselves, include *Osmunda regalis*

When it is grown in dappled shade, Nectaroscordum siculum will seed itself with ease. This delicately coloured plant has attractive flowers of lime green with pink and claret detailing.

(royal fern), *Matteuccia struthiopteris* (shuttlecock fern) and *Dryopteris dilatata* (broad buckler fern). All can reach 1.5m (5ft) or over.

But for summer, *Digitalis purpurea* (foxgloves) will colonize the shaded garden with purple, lilac and white spikes, and *D. lutea* will have 1m (3ft) creamy spires. Provided you have space as well as damp soil, the rodgersias offer some magnificent plants. *Rodgersia pinnata* 'Elegans' has deeply divided, bronze-tinted leaves and pink spikes of flowers growing to about 90cm (36in). When it is mixed with blue hosta foliage, the contrast is remarkable, while white Japanese anemones like *A. × hybrida* 'Luise Uhink' would brighten the area in late summer. I also like *Rodgersia aesculifolia* 'Irish Bronze', which has coarsely crinkled, leathery brown foliage and cream flowers. Link this with white *Astilbe* 'Silberlicht' and, for late summer, a mass of the elegant *Tricyrtis hirta,* which has unusual white-spotted, purple flowers above hairy leaves and grows to about 1m (3ft). Astilbes, like hostas, are among the finest of the shade-loving plants, and they associate well with white astrantias or *Miscanthus sinensis* 'Variegatus', an ornamental grass.

Hostas, however, are the traditional associates of astilbes, along with day lilies if the light is reasonable. New cultivars are being produced at a great rate. You should check their ultimate size. The bluer hostas are sought for silver and pastel schemes, but they work equally effectively if mixed with the bronzed rodgersia or astilbe foliage.

Colour in dappled shade Yellow flowers, like the globe flowers (*Trollius* varieties), or the yellow to orange-red *Mimulus luteus* (musk), will also grow in damp dappled shade, and there are, of course, yellow hostas, most of which are subject to sunburn and definitely prefer shade.

In early summer the elegant fronds of Matteuccia struthiopteris *(shuttlecock fern) rise from among rodgersia, hosta and lysichiton, all growing in damp shade.*

The beautiful leaves of the hostas associate well with *Acanthus mollis* in semi-shade. This plant is a statuesque 1.2m (4ft) high, and it has mauve and white flower spikes. Alternatively, *Aruncus dioicus* (goat's beard) is another imposing plant of 1.8m (6ft) or more. Add *Aconitum carmichaelii* 'Arendsii', a deep blue monkshood, a late summer-flowering plant, or *A.* 'Spark's Variety', which is violet and flowers earlier.

Other taller herbaceous plants for damp sites are the ligularias, which tolerate some sun as well as semi-shade and whose magnificently glossily rounded purple-green leaves provide summer-long interest. In light shade and rich, moist soil the ligularia would be the dominant focus of a group of plants, which could contain *Trollius chinensis* 'Golden Queen', with orange bowl flowers in midsummer up to 90cm (36in), and a mass of bright green ferns such as *Polystichum aculeatum* and the ground-covering *Tellima grandiflora* Rubra Group. The small meadowsweet,

Filipendula ulmaria 'Aurea' is grown for its rich golden foliage rather than its flowers. Reaching to about 50cm (20in), it must have some shade or it will burn. It is charming allied with a mass of brown grass from New Zealand, the 30cm (12in) tall *Uncinia uncinata*, and perhaps a few white astilbes.

For later in the year the cimicifugas are quite outstanding plants for semi-shade. The huge *C. simplex* 'Prichard's Giant' needs more light than most others and must have a lot of space for the tall, creamy spires, which reach 2.1m (7ft). There is a dark purple-leaved form, *C. simplex* 'Brunette', which is smaller and more arching, while *C. s.* 'White Pearl' requires more shade and is quite beguiling when massed. The former, being so large, is outstanding with *Astilboides tabularis* (syn. *Rodgersia tabularis*), which has vast, rounded, lotus-like green leaves from which tall, slim wands support drooping clusters of creamy star-like flowers.

In light shade Anemone × hybrida *'Honorine Jobert' is invaluable. It reproduces easily, and the white flowers last for weeks.*

If the shade area is acidic, grow the remarkable *Kirengeshoma palmata* with its graceful, creamy yellow, waxen, dangling flowers in late summer. The foliage is elegantly maple-like, and the plant reaches approximately 90cm (3ft) in height. Below this, the delicate butter yellow grass *Milium effusum* 'Aureum' or *Luzula sylvatica* 'Aurea' would emphasize the flowers.

Damp shade is ideal for candelabra primulas, mingling here with hostas and trollius.

DESIGN FOR A SHADED GARDEN

This corner of the garden is 8.5m (27ft) long by 3.75m (12ft) at its widest. The beds are 2m (6ft) and 2.5m (8ft) deep. The corner faces north and as this is a low part of the site, the soil is always damp. The longer bed does have some sunlight at the end of the day, and this extended the planting opportunities.

The soil is slightly acidic over a clay base. It had to be thoroughly turned over, aerated and conditioned before planting. Bulky rotted horse manure

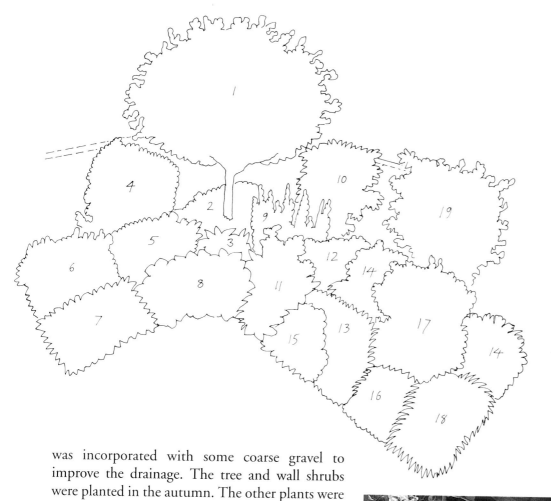

Key to plants
1. *Sorbus cashmiriana* (rowan)
2. *Dryopteris filix-mas* (fern)
3. *Arum pictum* (arum lily)
4. *Euonymus fortunei* 'Silver Queen'
5. *Dryopteris erythrosora* (fern)
6. *Astilbe × arendsii* 'Fanal'
7. *Epimedium perralderianum*
8. *Hosta undulata* var. *albomarginata* (syn. *H.* 'Thomas Hogg')
9. *Digitalis purpurea* Excelsior Hybrids (foxglove)
10. *Parthenocissus henryana*
11. *Rodgersia podophylla*
12. *Euphorbia amygdaloides* var. *robbiae* (spurge)
13. *Carex elata* 'Aurea' (Bowles' golden sedge)
14. *Anemone × hybrida* 'Honorine Jobert'
15. *Primula alpicola*
16. *Saxifraga fortunei* 'Rubrifolia'
17. *Aruncus dioicus* (goat's beard)
18. *Carex oshimensis* 'Evergold'
19. *Rosa* 'Félicité Perpétue'

The jagged leaves of Rodgersia podophylla *distinguish it from other plants in the lightly shaded, damp border.*

was incorporated with some coarse gravel to improve the drainage. The tree and wall shrubs were planted in the autumn. The other plants were put in the following spring.

The tree, *Sorbus cashmiriana*, provides the focus, growing to just under 10m (30ft) and after six years the canopy is nearly as wide. Other structure plants are a variegated evergreen, *Euonymus fortunei* 'Silver Queen', trained against the fence, and two climbers, *Parthenocissus henryana* and *Rosa* 'Félicité Perpétue'. Early in the year, *Euphorbia amygdaloides* var. *robbiae* and the evergreen epimedium provide ground cover.

The colours are white, cream, yellow and green with occasional reds like the neat red astilbe. *Aruncus dioicus* produces large, foamy cream flowers in summer, and by the end of the season the pure white flowers of *Anemone × hybrida* take us through until autumn, when the reddish carpeting saxifrage flowers last almost to the end of the year.

DESIGN FOR A HOT GRAVELLED GARDEN

The plants chosen for this sunny site share a need for well-drained soil that is reasonably moisture retaining and fertile. If the sub-soil is sandy, add bulky rotted compost. If it is clay, pierce with a fork and add sharp grit and rotted fibrous compost. If it is not free-draining, add fine coarse gravel in a layer no more than 7.5cm (3in) thick. Fine gravel is best, but choose rounded pea gravel if children use the garden. Otherwise, a coarser variety of gravel chippings is better because these chips do not roll about so much. Select a colour of gravel that blends, not contrasts, with the style of the garden.

The advantages of gravel gardens are many. This design provides for random shapes and planting. Borders are not relevant and gravel helps to suppress weeds, conserve moisture and keep plant roots fairly cool. Many plants will seed themselves in gravel, which adds informal charm.

The plants used here associate well because they share the same requirements.

The backing shrubs are all sun-lovers and provide foliage and flowers for the summer. Stachys, diascia and artemisia are low and spreading. Agapanthus and linum provide late summer flowers, while helianthum, anthemis and diascia display flowers at a low level for a long time.

The grasses, one a dark brown-red, two fine and silvery, add character to the plan.

A scheme like this is easy to maintain and looks attractive through summer.

A gravel mulch suppresses weeds and retains moisture, to the benefit of these sun-loving flowers. Hot yellow genista, flaming red poppies, violas and alliums provide colour among grey and silver foliage.

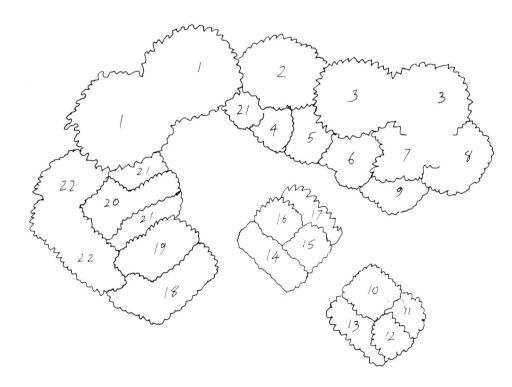

Key to plants
1. *Lavatera assurgentiflora* 'Barnsley'
2. *Hebe salicifolia* 'Snow Wreath'
3. *Cistus purpureus*
4. *Helianthemum* 'Wisley Primrose'
5. *Agapanthus* Headbourne Hybrids
6. *Carex* 'Frosted Curls'
7. *Carex buchananii*
8. *Stachys byzantina* 'Silver Carpet'
9. *Helianthemum* 'Fire Dragon'
10. *Diascia vigilis*
11. *Anthemis punctata* ssp. *cupaniana*
12. *Sedum spathulifolium* 'Cape Blanco'
13. *Linum narbonense*
14. *Sedum spurium* 'Atropurpureum'
15. *Artemisia stelleriana* 'Mori' (syn. 'Boughton Silver')
16. *Stipa tenuissima*
17. *Iris* 'Red Heart'
18. *Dianthus* 'Lilian'
19. *Lavandula stoechas*
20. *Parahebe catarractae* (blue form)
21. *Tulbaghia violacea*
22. *Euphorbia griffithii* 'Dixter'

10 • A DASH OF HERBS

Opposite: *Purple sage leaves set off the intensely magenta alliums and slightly paler flowers of the lavender. Behind them is a mass of deep red-bronze fennel.*

Herbs are the founder members of the art of gardening. Early recognition of their medicinal and culinary value meant that horticultural expertise was acquired, and the growing of herbs became an essential ingredient in many European gardens. The early 'farming' methods employed by the monasteries emphasized parallel linear plots for easy harvesting. This eventually led to geometric patterns and thence to the charms of the knot gardens. By the mid-seventeenth century Culpeper was adding to the writings of Gerard and

Verbena bonariensis *and parsley grow behind a Burford cloche.*

Parkinson, but insisting on using English names rather than Latin to popularize these plants and to remove some of the academic mystique associated with them.

Over subsequent centuries the interest in herbs waxed and waned, but today they are in vogue, for preserving (not just food but the skin), for the charms of pot pourris and the rediscovery of organic dyes.

In the contemporary summer garden, summer days are redolent with aromatic fragrances thickened with herbal nuance. Lavenders mix with verbena, with sage and with thyme to inspire nostalgia and a sense of times gone by.

Herbs can be used in the summer garden in many different ways. Their appeal is subtle, the flowers are not flashy, colours tend to be restrained, but habit is not. Many are tall and many are rambling.

The formal herb garden

If you decide to grow herbs in a traditional period style of garden then you will need to devise a layout divided with paths and probably edged with low hedging or edging plants. The whole could be hedged in yew, fuchsia or *Rosa rugosa*. You would want to include seats nestling among scents, possibly features like a bird bath and maybe a pergola or arbour, acknowledging the herb garden as a place of summer enchantment, a place for stirring the senses. You might include the apothecary rose, *Rosa gallica* var. *officinalis*, or the sweet briar, *Rosa eglanteria* as romantic partners, or clipped bays, *Laurus nobilis*, to add form to the scheme. The beds might be circular or rectangular, or you may decide to create more abstract shapes.

It is important to recognize that many herbs are invasive, however, and many are wayward. Having no social conscience, they will not hesitate to take out the opposition. The invasive mints, *Mentha* varieties, *Myrrhis odorata* (sweet cicely), *Melissa officinalis* (lemon balm), *Cochlearia armoracia* (horseradish) and *Cichorum intybus* (chicory) should all be sited in an informal part of the herb garden firmly contained by paths. Some, like the mints, could be confined to containers, where they will be attractive and available but not anti-social.

Others spread their favours by prolific seed distribution. If they are easy to weed, like *Alchemilla mollis* (lady's mantle) and *Tanacetum parthenium* (syn. *Chrysanthemum parthenium*; feverfew), then the random distribution can be extremely charming. But some are large plants, and you will not want an excess, so beware when they dispose of their seeds in the manner of *Oenthera biennis* (evening primrose), *Impatiens balsamina* (balsam) and *Angelica archangelica* (angelica). Many would be welcome to rove in wilder areas. *Borago officinalis* (borage) has pretty hairy blue flowers, *Euphorbia lathyris* (caper spurge) is a stylish biennial that will do well in shade and *Anthricus cerefolium* (chervil) is a lacy member of the Umbelliferae family, as is *Conium maculatum* (hemlock), the poison from which Socrates died.

Low hedging is the traditional way of containing your herb garden. *Lavandula* (lavender) may be clipped in late spring and again after flowering. *Santolina chamaecyparissus* (cotton lavender) is also traditionally used for silver-grey low hedging. *Teucrium chamaedrys* (germander),

Above: *The clipped standard holly,* Ilex × merserveae *'Blue Prince', stands above the pink* Lavandula angustifolia *'Loddon Pink' and variegated apple mint.*

Right: Myrrhis odorata, *commonly known as sweet cicely, is a herb that does well in light shade. It has a distinctive aniseed flavour.*

Hyssopus officinalis (hyssop) and the romantic *Nepeta racemosa* (syn. *N. mussinii*) will all serve as effective low hedges, adding aromatic foliage.

If you prefer to edge, rather than hedge, *Allium schoenoprasum* (chives) have grass-like foliage and pretty flowers. The smaller flowering dianthus and geraniums will also suit. *Alchemilla mollis* (lady's mantle) is less neat as summer progresses, and tends to seed rampantly, but it is a charming and informal edger.

For summer planting of a formal scheme, aim for fragrance plus visual effect. Ordinary *Thymus vulgaris* or the variegated *T. × citriodorus* will add scents to the air and provide low-level planting to enhance the grey, purple and yellow sages. There are also assorted carpet thymes. The leaves of golden marjoram are as colourful as buttercups, and the pretty *Dianthus caryophyllus,* known also as gillyflower (clove pinks), add delicate spots of pink.

A pot of salsify is surrounded by wild strawberries. Behind are chives in flower.

Symphytum ×
uplandicum *(Russian
comfrey) grows here with*
Phlomis fruticosa
*(Jerusalem sage), lavender,
chives and golden
marjoram.*

(bergamot) provide bright colours, and the stems of *Rumex sanguineus* (bloody dock) are a vivid scarlet, while the dark wine red foliage of *Atriplex hortensis* 'Purpurea' (Swiss chard) can be very effective. Even the leaves of *Ocimum basilicum* (annual sweet basil) have a purple-red tinge to them.

Herbs among the perennials

Many herbs are so decorative and subtle that associating them with more floriferous colleagues for the summer can be very effective.

My particular favourites, the sub-shrub sages, *Salvia officinalis* cultivars, seem to be in accord with every situation. The simple common sage rarely flowers, but the leaves are a soft dove grey, amenable to many summer schemes. Grey sages work well with other silver foliage and with whites; they can also be very appealing with cream colours, like the plumes of *Filipendula hexapetala* or the pale primrose daisies of *Anthemis tinctoria* 'Wargrave'.

It is worth looking for *Salvia lavandulifolia*, a Spanish sage noted for its lavender-blue spikes of flowers in high summer and very strong perfume. Variegated forms of sage are also available, and are just as adaptable to mixed planting as their plainer siblings. *Salvia officinalis* 'Icterina' has leaves that are light green flushed with yellow, which will enhance gold schemes without being coarse.

Purple sage is one of the plants that I use in nearly all garden schemes. This sage has purple-grey velvet foliage, further blessed with violet-blue flowers. It is in a subtle class of its own, a fine plant, which settles well into more or less any colour scheme. Try it with the yellow dandelion-like plant *Hieracium villosum* (hawkweed), or its invasive burnt orange relative *Pilosella aurantiaca* (syn. *H. aurantiacum*) and the pure orange *Geum* 'Borisii' for an eye-catching contrast. Or try it instead of the silver-grey of lamb's tongue or cotton lavender as a foil for roses. Less adaptable, but very pretty, is the highly variegated form of

Most herbs, however, are taller and many have a distinctive habit. The beauties of the hazy *Foeniculum vulgare* (fennel), which by midsummer may reach 1.5m (5ft), are prized. Both the green and the bronze forms add the same insubstantial foliage quality as the asparagus fern. They are responsive to every breath of air and provide a foil for more strident plants like the columnar *Verbascum thapsus* (mullein), or the expansive *Inula helenium* (elecampane), with its huge leaves and golden flowers. *Anethum graveolens* (dill) and *Artemisia absinthium* (wormwood) also have ultra-fine foliage but at a lower height of 90cm (3ft).

Colour in herbs is usually subtle; the bronze of the fennel and the pink, white or lime-green hues of many of the flowers are restrained. However, annual nasturtiums, pot marigolds, *Hypericum perforatum* (St John's wort) and *Monarda didyma*

Hazy fennel creates a soft image in the summer border.

sage, *Salvia officinalis* 'Tricolor', which, as its name indicates, is three-coloured, grey-green, white and pink. Though very prettily evergreen, like the others, it is not quite as strong but does have a neat habit.

Particularly fragrant, but regrettably a tender plant, is pineapple sage, *Salvia elegans* 'Scarlet Pineapple' (syn. *S. rutilans*), which is truly scented of pineapples. It makes a smallish bush with vivid scarlet flowers in late summer. If you have a sunny protected site I recommend it.

Another herb, planted for looks as well as utility, is rosemary. These pretty, delicate shrubs flower in late spring and then settle down to providing a modest evergreen backing. Although *Rosmarinus officinalis* 'Miss Jessopp's Upright', grows with a narrow upright habit, it provides formality among rounder shapes. This is a hardy shrub, which will need occasional pruning or tying

in if it begins to splay. *R. officinalis* Prostratus Group is also a blessing, as the plant trails down and follows the contour of the bank or wall in the same manner as *Cotoneaster dammeri*. To my regret it is not able to cope with frost.

Bay is, of course, the other important 'designer' shrub-herb. It is really a tree but responds to clipping, even to the point of topiary, and it is usually restricted it to sculptured forms in the formal herb garden, or confined to large clay pots in stylishly shaped lollipops. However, within the mixed border, bay may be grown as a simple dark evergreen mass, backing a planting bed for summer perennials. This culinary herb is hardy in temperate areas once it is established.

Foeniculum vulgare (fennel) is also used as a decorative plant as well as being grown for its culinary virtues. The tall, feathery, insubstantial form fraternizes well with more precisely shaped plants. A mass of hazy green fennel among *Aconitum* 'Ivorine' (white monkshood), *Astrantia major* ssp. *involucrata* 'Shaggy' and the late-flowering *Cimicifuga racemosa* would lighten the picture.

The bronze-foliaged fennel is also attractive, and is well suited to lighter coloured or variegated shrubs. You could consider planting it with luminous pale blues, like *Veronica gentianoides* for early summer, and *Iris sibirica* 'Heavenly Blue' to be followed in midsummer by the tall yellow tree lupin, *Lupinus arboreus*. This is about the same height as the bronze fennel, and you must allow space for such a combination.

For more moderate herb foliage that looks well with summer plants, *Anthemis nobilis* (camomile) has a pretty ground-level foliage, which will stay green through the year, and has white daisies in summer. *Allium schoenoprasum* (chives) provides clumps of round lilac-pink flowers with small, reedy leaves. *Santolina chamaecyparissus* (cotton lavender) makes clipped ever-grey mounds, as does the silvery *Helichrysum italicum* (syn. *angustifolium*; curry plant). These are useful as hedging, but are effective clumped in groups of three or more. The scented-leaved *Melissa officinalis* (lemon balm) may be found in golden form, like *Origanum vulgare* 'Aureum' (golden marjoram). *Mentha requenii*

Low lighting makes this herb and perennial garden attractive. The centrepiece sundial is surrounded by a green, mossy-textured camomile lawn.

(Corsican mint) can provide low ground-cover and is less rampantly adventurous than other mints.

Alchemilla mollis (lady's mantle) has particularly beautiful rounded leaves and will grow anywhere and everywhere. But for colourful foliage, golden marjoram and the intensely blue rue, *Ruta graveolens*, are truly outstanding.

Try, too, siting the attractive tree onion, *Allium cepa* Proliferum Group, with the branching grey-leaved *Lychnis coronaria* Alba Group and *Thymus serpyllum* at the foot.

Although the flowers of most herbs are subdued, some carry flowers. *Monarda didyma* (bergamot) has richly red or pink flowers; *M.* 'Adam' has crimson ones, and *M.* 'Croftway Pink' is a good pink. *Verbascum thapsus* (mullein) has very tall yellow spikes, *Inula helenium* (elecampane) has tousled chrome daisies, and, of course, *Calendula officinalis* (pot marigold) is nearly orange.

This does not mean that the more subdued or subtle flowers are not pretty or useful for a border. The hairy-leaved *Borago officinalis* (borage) has delicate, star-like, azure-blue flowers from early to midsummer. For ground-cover, particularly under trees, the smaller *Symphytum grandiflorum* (comfreys) have pretty combinations of blue-pink and brown-cream modest flowers, which begin in late spring but last into early summer. The very pretty purple and yellow flowers of *Viola tricolor* (heartsease) will continue to flower throughout the growing season.

Two blues must be included. The first is that of the flaxes: the annual common flax of wild linen fame, *Linum usitassimum*, with its slim wands, above which pale blue, saucer-shaped flowers appear for two months in summer, and the form *Linum narbonense*, which is prettier and sturdier. *L. n.* 'June Perfield' is one that should be sought. The other delicate blue is that of *Nepeta* (catmint), which again has a garden form worth securing. This is *Nepeta* 'Six Hills Giant', a particularly captivating summer plant.

Containers

Herbs that are desirable but in need of real restraint, like the invasive mints, are best grown in containers. Others that are not very hardy are also better grown in movable containers that can be put outside for the summer season. *Ocimum basilicum* (basil) and its purple counterpart are tender, so is *Petroselinum crispum* (parsley), with its densely curled, moss-like texture. *Artemisia dracunculus* (French tarragon) is difficult to establish and tender. Its slim leaves, on a stem almost 80cm (30in) long, would look very attractive grown with *Thymus* × *citriodorus* (lemon thyme) and brilliant tumbling nasturtiums.

Green fennel merges with the cream flower spikes of Digitalis lutea *(foxglove).*

127

DESIGN FOR A HERB GARDEN

This formal herb garden is 8m (26ft) by 7m (23ft). On three sides it is enclosed with hedges of raspberries, gooseberries and *Rosa rugosa*. Traditional low hedges of box and santolina divide them into compartments. Two bay trees, topiaried as lollipops, a matching pair of fastigiate yews and upright rosemary bushes emphasize the symmetry. Such a tightly organized scheme is ideal for a herb garden. The main frame of the garden is square, but terracotta tiles laid at 45 degrees provide a contrast. The unit size of the tiles is 30cm (12in) square and the red blends with the soft colours of the herbs.

Herbs require a sunny site. Perennials like lavender, bay and rosemary can

Opposite: Thymus *'Silver Posie' carpets the ground, mixing well with* Sedum spathulifolium *and sempervivums.*

be purchased in containers, as established plants. Then a quick effect can be achieved if other pot-grown plants are bought from the nursery. Many herbs are easily grown from seed. Here they may be scattered on a fine soil tilth or sown in drills and covered lightly with soil. This can be done in spring or in autumn as long as there is no frost.

The plan provides culinary herbs, but the emphasis is more upon the subtle attractions of soft colour, textural pattern and aromatic foliage. Violas, comfrey, lady's mantle, catmint and alliums provide flower colour, garnished with annual nasturtiums and marigolds. Foliage colour comes from the gold and purple sages, bronze fennel and from carpet thymes. Texture effects are found in the chives, sages, fennel and santolina. Scents are a large part of the charm of the herb garden and come from foliage like that of the lemon balm, scented geraniums, catmint, thymes, rosemary and the many mints.

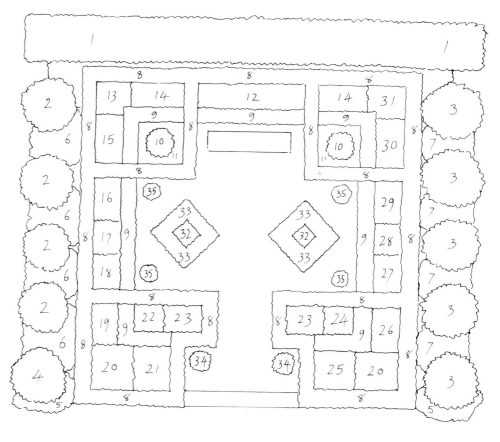

Key to plants

1. *Rosa* 'Fru Dagmar Hastrup'
2. Raspberries
3. Gooseberries
4. *Taxus baccata* 'Fastigiata' (yew)
5. *Geranium macrorrhizum*
6. *Alchemilla mollis* (lady's mantle)
7. *Nepeta racemosa* (syn. *N. mussinii;* catmint)
8. *Buxus sempervirens* 'Suffruticosa' (dwarf box)
9. *Santolina chamaecyparissus*
10. *Laurus nobilis* (bay)
11. *Allium schoenoprasum* (chives)
12. *Allium giganteum*
13. *Foeniculum vulgare* (bronze fennel)
14. *Lavandula angustifolia* (lavender)
15. *Salvia officinalis* 'Icterina' (golden sage)
16. *Borago officinalis* (borage)
17. *Thymus vulgaris* (thyme)
18. *Satureja montana* (winter savory)
19. *Melissa officinalis* (lemon balm)
20. *Rosmarinus officinalis* (rosemary)
21. *Origanum vulgare* (marjoram)
22. *Mentha suaveolens* (syn. *M. rotundifolia;* apple mint)
23. *Tropaeolum* spp. (nasturtiums)
24. *Mentha × piperita citrata* (eau-de-Cologne mint)
25. *Ocimum basilicum* (basil)
26. *Symphytum officinale* (comfrey)
27. *Artemisia dracunculus* (French tarragon)
28. *Salvia officinalis* (sage)
29. *Anthriscus cerefolium* (chervil)
30. *Salvia officinalis* Purpurascens Group (purple sage)
31. *Angelica archangelica* (angelica)
32. *Viola tricolor* (heartease)
33. *Thymus serpyllum* (carpet thyme)
34. *Petroselinum crispum* (parsley)
35. *Calendula officinalis*

PLANT LISTS

Following are the names of plants that are lovely in the summer garden.

TREES

Aralia elata
JAPANESE ANGELICA TREE
Small
A large, suckering shrub or small tree. Large bipinnate leaves gathered in ruff-like arrangements towards the tip of the stem. White flowers are produced in large panicles in early autumn. Avoid clay or poorly drained soils.

Betula pendula 'Golden Cloud'
Medium
A deciduous, golden-leafed variety of the white-stemmed, broadly columnar tree with pendulous branchlets. Relatively surface rooting. Hardy. Plant in sun or semi-shade in any moist but well drained soil.

Cercidiphyllum japonicum
KATSURA TREE
Medium
A deciduous, spherical-crowned tree with slender, sometimes multi-stemmed branches. Grown for its foliage and spectacular autumn colour. Small heart-shaped leaves similar to those of *Cercis siliquastrum* emerge bright pinkish then sea green, turning smoky pink, red or yellow in autumn. Colours best on lime-free soil. Grows in deep, moist fertile soil in sun or semi-shade.

Cornus 'Eddie's White Wonder'
Small
Large white bracts appearing in late spring. Mid-green oval leaves turning red and purple in autumn.

Fraxinus sieboldiana
FLOWERING ASH
Small
Compact deciduous tree. Fully hardy but very slow growing. Clusters of small fragrant, star-shaped creamy white flowers in early summer. Needs sun and fertile, well-drained soil. Tolerant of smoke-polluted areas and coastal situations.

Koelreuteria paniculata
PRIDE OF INDIA OR GOLDEN RAIN TREE
Medium
A broad-headed tree with pinnate leaves. Upright yellow panicles in July/August are followed by bronzy bladder-like fruits. The leaves turn yellow in autumn. Flowers best in hot dry summers.

SHRUBS

Acer
Acer palmatum
JAPANESE MAPLE
Large
Rounded, deciduous bushy-headed shrub, spreading with age. Large palmate leaves, 5- or 7-lobed, turning red, orange and yellow in autumn. Fully hardy but prefers sheltered situations. Tolerant of some lime but the following cultivars require neutral or lime-free soil with plenty of humus.

A. p. 'Bloodgood'
Large
Deciduous, bushy headed shrub with deep reddish-purple palmate leaves that turn brilliant red in autumn. Small reddish flowers in mid-spring are often followed by decorative, winged red fruits. Fully hardy. Shelter from strong winds.

A.p. 'Linearilobum Atropurpureum'
Large
Leaves deeply cut to the base and autumn colour.

A.p. 'Osakazuki'
Large
Finely toothed, green leaved palmate that turns to brilliant scarlet in autumn.

A.p. 'Senkaki'
CORAL BARK MAPLE
Large
More erect than others in this group. Bright coral red stems are striking in winter. Small palmate leaves, orange-yellow in spring, green in summer turning gold in autumn. This cultivar is also sold as A.p. 'Sango-kaku'.

Caryopteris × clandonensis
BLUE SPIRAEA
Small
Rounded bush with low, arching branches, grown for its greyish-green, aromatic foliage and freely produced blue flower spikes borne in autumn. Frost hardy. Prefers full sun and light, well-drained soil.

Ceanothus 'Italian Skies'
CALIFORNIAN LILAC
Medium
A vigorous evergreen shrub with low or cascading habit. Dark green leaves with abundant blue flowers. There are many other excellent varieties, some of which are deciduous and half-hardy. Requires full sun and good drainage.

Cercis canadensis 'Forest Pansy'
Large
A very wide spreading shrub with rich plum-purple foliage.

Cistus 'Silver Pink'
ROCK ROSE
Small
Grey evergreen foliage with pink single flowers in early summer. See also *C. × hybridus* (syn. *C. × corbariensis*) and *C. ladanifer.*

Cornus kousa var. chinensis
Large
An elegant deciduous shrub. Leaves with undulating margins turn bronze in autumn. Grown

for its 'flowers', which are really white bracts, about 8cm (3in) across on upright stalks in summer above spreading, tiered branches. Requires well-drained soil; dislikes shallow chalky soil. Plant in full sun to part shade.

Hydrangea

Medium to large deciduous flowering, bushy shrubs. In mid- to late summer blue or purple flowers are produced in acid soil with a pH of up to 5.5. In neutral or alkaline soils flowers are pink or red. White flowers are not affected by pH. Prefers moist but well-drained, manured soil and a sheltered site in sun or partial shade. Frost hardy. *H. macrophylla* is a Japanese species which is divided into two groups. Lacecaps have flat, open heads with fertile flowers in the centre and larger sterile flowers on the outer rim. Mopheads, which are also known as hortensias, have domed, dense, mostly sterile flower heads.

H. m. 'Geoffrey Chadbund' Lacecap

Medium

Large brick-red florets around central small light red flowers. Acidic soils tend to deepen the colour to dark red-purple.

H. m. 'Mariesii Perfecta' (syn. H. m. 'Blue Wave') Lacecap

Medium

Vigorous grower, pink or blue large plate-like heads, the outer ring pink (blue on acid soil) with purplish-blue central florets.

Hydrangea macrophylla

H. m. 'Générale Vicomtesse de Vibraye' Hortensia

Medium

Rose pink or sky blue flowers. Early to flower. Prefers shade.

H. quercifolia

OAK-LEAVED HYDRANGEA

Large

A tender shrub of loose habit with deeply scalloped dark green leaves, which produce good autumn colour. The greeny-white flowers are produced on erect panicles in summer and turn purple with age.

Lavandula stoechas

FRENCH LAVENDER

Small

A hardy, evergreen, bushy shrub with aromatic grey-green, linear leaves. Spikes of fragrant, deep purple tubular flowers, with tufts, of purple bracts topping each flower spike, appear from late spring to early summer.

Philadelphus
Philadelphus 'Manteau d'Hermine'

Small

A compact but bushy shrub. Clusters of double creamy-white, vanilla-scented flowers appear amid small pale to mid-green leaves from early to midsummer.

P. coronarius 'Aureus'

Medium

An upright deciduous shrub with oval, medium sized leaves, which are bright yellow in spring to early summer, later changing to greenish-yellow. Clusters of very fragrant, creamy white, four-petalled flowers appear in early summer. Retains its colour best if grown in semi-shade.

P. c. 'Variegatus'

Medium

Same as above but with slightly larger leaves, which have irregular creamy white margins. Highly fragrant. Cream flowers late spring to early summer.

Pittosporum
Pittosporum 'Garnettii'

Medium

An evergreen, rather slow-growing columnar shrub of dense, bushy habit grown for its ornamental foliage. Rounded grey-green leaves edged with creamy white becoming tinged with deep pink in cold areas. May bear greenish-purple flowers spring to summer. Does best in mild areas. Needs a well-drained, fairly light soil.

Philadelphus coronarius 'Aureus'

Pittosporum tenuifolium 'Irene Paterson'

Same as above but leaves are mottled with grey-green on an almost white leaf.

Salvia
Salvia officinalis 'Icterina'
GOLDEN SAGE
Small
A compact evergreen shrub with aromatic grey-green leaves variegated with yellow. Prefers sun and well-drained soil.

S. o. Purpurascens Group
PURPLE-LEAVED SAGE
Small
As above but with greyish-purple leaves. Violet-purple flowers are freely produced on reddish-purple stems.

Salvia officinalis Purpurascens Group

Santolina chamaecyparissus
COTTON LAVENDER
Small
An evergreen hummock-shaped shrub with dense, aromatic, grey-white felted stems and filigree leaves. The abundant yellow, button-shaped flowers are produced in mid- to late summer on two-year-old wood. Prune hard in spring to promote strong growth. Requires sun and well-drained but not too rich soil. Look also for *S.c.* 'Lemon Queen', which has light yellow flowers, and *S. pinnata* ssp. *neapolitana* 'Sulphurea' which has green foliage.

Viburnum
Deciduous and evergreen shrubs offering a great variety of form, flower, fragrance, fruit and seasonal changes.

V. davidii
Small
A small evergreen shrub of compact habit. The large, narrowly oval, glossy dark green leathery leaves are three-veined. The small white flowers are followed by bright blue berry clusters on female plants when plants of both sexes are planted in groups, ensuring cross-pollination.

V. × rhytidophylloides
Large
A fast-growing evergreen shrub with big corrugated green leaves. Creamy white flowers are followed by red fruits which turn to black. It is necessary to have plants of both sexes in close proximity for fruiting.

V. tinus
LAURUSTINUS
Large
A dense bushy evergreen shrub with oval dark green leaves. Freely produced flat heads of small white blooms open from pink buds during late winter and spring. Copes with shade, cold wind and moist soil conditions.

FOLIAGE

Artemisia
Artemisia absinthium 'Lambrook Silver'
WORMWOOD
Small
A silvery form with aromatic silky dissected leaves. Needs protection in an exposed site.

A. alba 'Canescens'
Small
A fully hardy dense ground-covering shrub with finely cut, silver-grey leaves. Semi-evergreen.

A. ludoviciana var. *latiloba*
WORMWOOD
Medium
A bushy shrub with aromatic lance-shaped, silvery-white leaves.

A. 'Powis Castle'
WORMWOOD
Medium
A hardy evergreen dome-shaped shrub with abundant, aromatic grey dissected leaves.

A. schmidtiana 'Nana'
Dwarf
A hardy evergreen dome-shaped shrub with finely divided silver-grey leaves. Requires a sandy soil.

Foeniculum vulgare
FENNEL
Medium
This fully hardy, upright perennial has fragrant, finely divided green leaves, which are freely produced on the branching stems. The yellowish-green flowers, produced in umbels, are followed by green seeds, which drop soon after turning yellow. Seeds freely, so remove flower heads after fading. Grow in open, sunny position in fertile, well-drained soil. *F. v.* 'Giant Bronze' is brownish-red.

Heuchera
Heuchera cylindrica 'Greenfinch'
Medium
Tall, well-formed spikes of olive green bells in midsummer.

H. micrantha var. *diversifolia* 'Palace Purple'
Small
An evergreen perennial forming large clumps of heart-shaped, deep red, serrated leaves. Numerous tiny white bell-shaped flowers are held high on wiry stems. Fully to frost hardy. Prefers a moisture-retentive but well-drained soil.

H. 'Pewter Moon'
Small
As above, but the green-purple leaves are blotched with grey.

H. 'Snow Storm'
Small
As above, but leaves are round scalloped-edged and almost entirely cream in summer, with dark green ruffled borders. Bright cerise, bell-shaped flowers in summer.

Heuchera micrantha var. *diversifolia* 'Palace Purple'

Hosta
Hosta fortunei var. albopicta
Medium
In spring loose scrolled leaves unfold to a bright butter yellow edged with green, which turns to soft green and olive in summer.

H. 'Ginko Craig'
Dwarf
A mound-forming dwarf variety with lance-shaped, white-edged leaves and mauve flowers.

H. 'Halcyon'
Small
As above, but with smaller more slender blue-grey leaves. Mauve flowers in summer.

H. 'Royal Standard'
Small
Abundant green foliage with white, sweetly scented flowers. Required good soil. Likes sun.

H. sieboldiana var. elegans
Small
Clumps of large, rounded heavily veined blue-grey leaves. Dense mauve flowers up to 1m (3ft) high are produced in summer. Best in light shade and not too dry soil.

H. undulata
Small
Rich green twisting leaves with lilac-purple flowers.

H. 'Zounds'
Small
A yellow-leaved hosta that copes well with sunny conditions.

Macleaya cordata
PLUME POPPY
Medium
An upright, fully hardy, clump-forming perennial with numerous buff-tinted, star-shaped flowers appearing on leafy spikes in late summer. It is grown for its large, deeply lobed, purple-greyish leaves. Plant in well-drained soil in sun or part shade. Spreads rapidly.

Melianthus major
HONEY BUSH
Medium
A half-hardy evergreen shrub with beautiful grey-green, deeply fingered and serrated leaves. Tubular brownish-red flowers with green stamens are produced in spring and summer. Flowers best on poor soil. The stems are very lax so they need support.

Stachys byzantina
LAMB'S TONGUE
Small
A vigorous but shallow-rooting evergreen ground cover with dense mats of woolly silvery coloured leaves. Look for *S. b.* 'Silver Carpet', which does not flower, and *S. b.* 'Primrose Heron', which is a golden-silver variety for early summer. Although it is fairly hardy, it may not survive in cold, wet or exposed situations.

PERENNIALS

Acanthus spinosus
BEAR'S BREECHES
Large
A large arching perennial with deeply cut and spiny glossy dark green leaves. Spires of funnel-shaped soft mauve and white flowers with green bracts are produced freely in summer. Grows best in sun or light shade in deep well-drained soil.

Achillea
Achillea × lewisii 'King Edward'
Dwarf
A semi-evergreen rounded perennial 10 × 23cm (4 × 9in). Feathery soft grey-green leaves bear compact heads of minute, pale yellow flower heads from spring to summer. Suitable for rock gardens. Requires full sun and slightly moisture-retentive soils.

A. 'Taygetea'
Small
An evergreen perennial with erect stems. Bears flat heads of lemon-yellow flowers throughout summer above clumps of feathery silver-grey leaves.

Aconitum
Aconitum carmichaelii 'Arendsii'
MONKSHOOD
Medium
Glossy, dark green, deeply divided leaves. The erect stems are topped in late summer to autumn with short spikes of deep amethyst blue flowers. Moist, rich soil, semi-shade or sun. May need staking.

A. 'Sparks Variety'
MONKSHOOD
Medium
A fully hardy perennial with widely branching stems and cut leaves. Deep violet-hooded flowers are produced in summer. Full sun to shade, moist soil preferred. Responds well to spring mulching. The cultivar A. 'Ivorine' bears cream flowers in early summer.

Alcea rosea
HOLLYHOCK
Large
A fully hardy biennial or short-lived perennial grown for its tall spikes of rosette-like single or double flowers, which are produced in various colours in summer and early autumn. Needs full sun to light shade and well-drained soil. A. r. 'Nigra' has very dark plum-purple single flowers.

Alcea rosea 'Nigra'

Allium
ORNAMENTAL ONION
Perennials with bulbs, rhizomes or fibrous root stocks. Most have slim onion-scented leaves. Flowers are usually dense globes or open umbels. Sunny situation. Good drainage. Eventually produce clumps and are best left undisturbed for several years. Collect the seed in autumn.

A. aflatunense
Bulb
Summer-flowering purple spheres of tiny flowers.

A. siculum (syn. Nectaroscordum siculum)
Bulb
Late spring to early summer. Pendant umbels of small green-purple bell flowers. Semi-shade. Naturalizes by seed or offsets.

Anchusa azurea 'Loddon Royalist'
Tall
Hardy with a spreading habit. Clusters of small, bell-shaped, gentian blue flowers are produced on hairy stems from early to late summer. The arching grey-green, lance-shaped leaves are covered in rough hairs.

Anemone
Anemone × hybrida
WINDFLOWER
These vigorous, fully hardy perennials have clumps of vine-shaped leaves and ascending, branching stems bearing shallowly cup-shaped flowers. Semi-shade to sun and well-drained soil. They flower in late summer.

A. × hybrida 'Luise Uhink'
Medium
Pure white, semi-double flowers.

A. × h. 'Königin Charlotte' (syn. 'Queen Charlotte')
Medium
Large semi-double rose pink flowers. Grows to 90cm (3ft) high.

A. hupehensis 'September Charm'
Medium
Dainty single soft pink flowers

Anthemis
Anthemis punctata ssp. cupaniana 'Nana'
Small
Evergreen, finely cut, silvery, aromatic foliage that turns green in winter. Small white daisy flowers with yellow stamens are borne singly on short stems in early summer. Remove dead flowers for repeat flowering.

A. tinctoria 'E.C. Buxton'
GOLDEN MARGUERITE
Medium
Carpeting clump-forming perennial, grown for its daisy-like flowers. Has masses of primrose yellow flowers on single stems in midsummer above a carpet of evergreen fern-like, crinkled mid-green leaves. Fully hardy. Easy to grow but likes a sunny open position and well-drained soil. Cut back after flowering for repeat flowering.

Astilbe
Hardy, summer-flowering perennials grown for their feathery, plume-like flower spikes, which are held well above dark green

fern-like foliage. Spent, dried and brown flowers remain on the plant well into winter. Needs moist, rich soil, prefers partial shade. Appreciates an annual spring mulch of well-rotted compost.

A. × *arendsii* 'Fanal'
Small
Feathery short spikes of tiny crimson red flowers. The leaves are mahogany-tinted in spring, turning dark green in summer.

A. × *arendsii* 'Snowdrift'
Medium
Free-flowering snow-white erect flower spikes above bright green foliage.

A. 'Sprite'
Dwarf
A clump-forming dwarf perennial has wide-branching sprays of feathery tapering plumes of tiny star-shaped shell-pink flowers in mid- to late summer. These are borne above broad dark green leaves which are divided into narrowly oval-toothed leaflets.

A. × *arendsii* 'Venus'
Tall
Pale pink flower plumes are held above broad dark green leaves which are divided into leaflets.

Astrantia major var. *rubra*
Medium
Wine red small shaggy flowers in mid- to late summer. White flowered and variegated varieties are available.

Brunnera macrophylla
Medium
Ground-covering perennial for soils that do not dry out. Sun or shade.

Has large, heart-shaped leaves. Sprays of blue flowers appear in late spring and early summer. *B. m.* 'Hadspen Cream' has variegated foliage and blue flowers.

Campanula
Campanula lactiflora
BELLFLOWER
Medium-tall
Light green ovate leaves are set all the way up the stems, which carry branching heads of deep lilac bell-shaped flowers. May need staking. Sun or light shade. Many forms, including white flowers and dwarf plants.

C. latifolia
GIANT BELLFLOWER
Large
A clump-forming perennial. Rounded mid-green basal leaves decrease in size up the long stalk, which terminates in many large, drooping, tubular, violet-blue or white flowers. Soil should not dry out. Sun or light shade.

C. persicifolia 'Telham Beauty'
BELLFLOWER
Medium
A long-flowering border perennial with evergreen rosettes of dark green leaves and slender wiry stems on which bells 2.5m (1in) wide, blue or white, cup-shaped flowers are produced close to the main stem. Sun or light shade.

Centranthus ruber
RED VALERIAN
Medium
A free-flowering perennial with fleshy gaucous green leaves and large long heads of small, star-shaped, deep pink flowers carried

in clusters above a long stem. *C. v.* var. *albus* is a white-flowering form.

Cephalaria gigantea
GREAT SCABIOUS
Large
A massive plant with dense clumps of dark green, divided leaves. Freely branched stems carry a succession of pale yellow pin-cushion shaped flowers. Requires a sunny position and ordinary soil.

Cimicifuga
Cimicifuga simplex 'Prichard's Giant' (syn. *C. ramosa*)
BUGBANE
Large
Slender strong stems carry feathery spikes of creamy white flowers above outstanding, deeply divided, striking foliage in late summer. The clumps become large in time and the leaves often turn yellow in autumn.

C. s. Atropurpurea Group
Large
Purplish leaves and stems with white arching racemes of fragrant flower spikes. Also available is *C. s.* 'Brunette'.

C. s. 'White Pearl'
Medium
The last to flower, with full arching wands of pure white flower heads in autumn. Smooth green and smaller divided foliage.

Coreopsis verticillata 'Moonbeam'
Small
A dense, erect plant with finely divided hair-like bright green leaves. Golden-yellow daisies are produced throughout summer.

Cosmos
Cosmos atrosanguineus (syn. *Bidens atrosanguinea*)
CHOCOLATE COSMOS
Medium
An upright perennial with very dark, maroon-crimson, chocolate-scented flower heads above slender stems. May be over-wintered if tuberous roots are protected with a deep mulch. Otherwise, grow as an annual.

C. bipinnatus
Annual
Medium
Daisy-shaped flowers of white, red, pink or orange with yellow centres are displayed on long flower stems during mid- to late summer. The leaves are fine and hazy. Needs sun and moist but well-drained soil. Will not thrive in very alkaline soil. May need staking.

Delphinium × *belladonna* Hybrids
Medium to tall
Great variety of colour from intense blue-purples to pastel pink-violets and pure white. Single-flowered. Must be staked.

Dendranthema Hybrids (syn. *Chrysanthemum*)
Medium
Formerly garden chrysanthemums. *D.* 'Clara Curtis' late summer, pink daisies; *D.* 'Emperor of China' is deep crimson and double-flowered in very late summer. Protect in winter. *D.* 'Duchess of Edinburgh' is bronze flowered and *D.* 'Mary Stoker' is yellow.

Dendranthema 'Nantyderry Sunshine'

Geranium

Many geraniums are of great garden value. Dwarf, medium and tall varieties are available, with colours from deep purple, pink, lilac, blue and white. Good foliage, some scented.

G. cinereum 'Ballerina'
Dwarf
A front of the border perennial with round grey-green leaves. Pale lilac-pink flowers feathered with crimson-purple are freely produced from spring until autumn.

G. phaeum 'Mourning Widow'
Medium
Small clump-forming, nodding purple-black flowers are produced in early summer on slender leafy stems. Copes with dry shade.

G. wallichianum 'Buxton's Variety'
Dwarf
This small, spreading perennial has a dense growth of silky green leaves and lavender-blue saucer-shaped flowers with large white centres and dark stamens throughout summer. Plant in reasonable, well-drained soil in sun or part shade.

Hemerocallis
DAY LILIES
Small to medium
Hardy, herbaceous, semi-evergreen perennials which form clumps of arching mid-green, strap-shaped leaves in summer and bear lily-like flowers from midsummer to early autumn. Sun or part shade, prefers good soil that is not too dry.

H. 'Bonanza'
Orange flowers with maroon centres.

H. 'Marion Vaughn'
Clear lemon yellow flowers, very vigorous.

H. 'Pink Damask'
Strong pink flowers.

H. 'Stafford'
Deep red flowers with orange yellow throats.

Iris
Irish chrysographes 'Black Knight'
Medium
A rhizomatous beardless iris producing 1–4 purple-black flowers with gold veining from late spring to early summer on branched stems. Narrow rush-like leaves. Moist soil.

I. germanica
COMMON GERMAN FLAG
Medium
A rhizomatous evergreen iris producing up to 6 scented, yellow bearded, blue-purple flowers in late spring, early summer. Needs good drainage, likes lime. Good forms include 'Black Swan' (nearly black flowers); 'Jane Phillips (light blue flowers) and 'Kent Pride' (deep brown and gold).

I. pallida 'Argentea Variegata'
DALMATIAN IRIS
An evergreen iris that produces 2–6 scented lilac blue flowers on strong branching stems. Grown for its variegated foliage. The leaves are blue-green striped with white. Sun to light shade.

Diascia rigescens
Small
A perennial with a low habit and shrubby growth, massed with narrow-toothed leaves. Long spikes of shell-like dusky, crimson-pink flowers are produced from late spring to early autumn. Not very hardy.

Euphorbia
Euphorbia characias ssp. wulfenii
SPURGE
Large
An evergreen upright perennial. The stems produce long, glaucous green lance-shaped leaves one year and spikes of yellow-green florets the following spring. Does best in sun or partial shade and well-drained soil. Needs a sheltered site in exposed areas. Its milky sap may irritate skin.

E. griffithii 'Fireglow'
SPURGE
Medium
A bushy perennial that bears glowing orange-red flowers in early summer. The lance-shaped leaves are mid-green with pale red midribs. Sun or partial shade.

I. sibirica
SIBERIAN IRIS
Medium
A fibrous-rooted, clump forming iris producing 2–3 dark veined blue to blue-purple flowers on branched stems above dark green strap-shaped leaves in late spring to early summer. Requires a sunny site in moist or boggy soil. Look for *I. s.* 'White Swirl' and *I. s.* 'Sky Wings'.

Knautia macedonia
Medium
A perennial with lax bushy grown. Basal clumps produce many curving stems, which carry pure dark crimson, double pincushion flowers measuring 5cm (2in) across.

Kniphofia
RED-HOT POKER
Fully to half-hardy perennial, which flowers from early to late summer depending on type. The flower stem rises above a clump of stiff grass-like leaves and produces poker-like spikes consisting of closely set down-ward-facing tubular flowers. Requires a sunny position in ordinary but well-drained soil.

K. 'Ada'
Medium
Upstanding spikes of bright orange-yellow are borne in summer.

K. 'Atlanta'
Medium
A hardy plant with heavy spikes of yellow and red above clumps of evergreen glaucous foliage. Does well in coastal areas.

Kniphofia 'Firefly'

K. 'Green Jade'
Medium
Slender spikes of jade green, with a hint of cream in late summer.

K. triangularis ssp. *triangularis* (syn. *K. galpinii*)
Medium
Soft orange-yellow dainty flower spikes held on wiry thin stems above clumps of green grass-like leaves.

Lathrys odoratus
SWEET PEA
Tall
A hardy, moderately fast-growing climbing annual that supports itself by means of tendrils. Single pairs by oval, mid-green leaves with highly scented pea-like pink, purple, blue or white flowers 2.5cm (1in) across.

Libertia formosa
Medium
An evergreen perennial with dark green grassy leaves. Branching sprays of small white saucer-shaped flowers with yellow stamens are produced in early summer. These are followed by orange seed pods.

Ligularia
Ornamental leaved plants with yellow or orange daisy-shaped flowers. Needs good but moist or even boggy soil and a sunny position.

L. dentata 'Desdemona'
Large
A perennial with large, rounded heart-shaped, brownish-green leaves, purplish beneath. Big branching stems terminate in large orange daisy-shaped flowers in late summer.

Ligularia dentata 'Desdemona'

L. 'The Rocket'
Large
Serrated, heart-shaped, dark green leaves produce nearly black stems, which each carry tall narrow spires of yellow flowers in late summer.

Lithodora diffusa 'Heavenly Blue' (syn. *Lithospermum diffusum*)
Alpine
Long display of deep blue flowers from mid- to late summer. Lime-free soil essential.

Lobelia cardinalis

Lobelia cardinalis
Large
A half-hardy, clump-forming perennial with purple stems and lance-shaped, purple leaves. Two-lipped bright red flowers appear in mid- to late summer. Needs damp soil and full sun. Good forms to look out for are *L.* 'Dark Crusader' with dark red flowers on long spikes in late summer to mid-autumn and *L.* 'Queen Victoria' with blazing red flowers. May need a heavy mulch in spring.

Nepeta 'Six Hills Giant'
CATMINT
Medium
A bushy plant with small aromatic leaves and sprays of lavender-coloured blooms from early summer until autumn. Requires sun and a well-drained soil.

Nicotiana sylvestris
TOBACCO PLANT
Tall and dwarf
A striking branching perennial, often grows as an annual in harsher climates. Fragrant flowers in late summer. Colours are white, lime green, pink and crimson.

Osteospermum 'Whirlgig'
An evergreen clump forming semi-woody perennial with a lax habit. Produces masses or single daisy-shaped bluish-white flowers with blue centres, whose pinched petals have a spoon-like appearance. The leaves are lance-shaped and grey-green. Best in warm areas or grown as an annual. Requires sun and well-drained soil.

Penstemon 'Sour Grapes'
Medium
A vigorous plant with large tubular grape-purple flowers born up the long stems in mid to late summer. The leaves are narrow and mid-green. Almost hardy when grown in a sunny site in well-drained soil fertile soil. Otherwise grow as bedding. *P.* 'Garnet' is garnet-red, *P.* 'Alice Hindley' is mid-blue with white.

Rodgersia aesculifolia 'Irish Bronze'
Large
A rhizomatous frost-hardy perennial. The dramatic purple-brown, crinkled leaves are held on sturdy purple stems. Creamy white, plume-shaped flowers are produced from midsummer. Requires good moist soil in sun or shade. Must not dry out.

Rudbeckia fulgida var. sullivantii 'Goldsturm'
BLACK-EYED SUSAN
Medium
An erect perennial with daisy-like warm yellow flowers and conical black centres, produced in late summer to autumn. Clumps of narrow, rough green leaves. Prefers moist soil in sun or shade. Reliable, easily grown plant.

Salvia
S. argentea
Small
Unusual silky grey leaves with white flowers in summer. Short-lived.

S. nemorosa 'East Friesland'
Small
Very reliable compact purple flowering plant.

Rudbeckia fulgida var. *sullivantii* 'Goldsturm'

S. pratensis Haematodes Group 'Indigo'
Large

A plant with dark green crinkled basal leaves. Leafless stems carry indigo blue flowers in midsummer. Needs sun and well-drained soil. Short-lived but spreads by seed.

S. × sylvestris 'May Night'
Large

A neat clump-forming perennial with narrow, rough, mid-green leaves. Indigo blue flower spikes in early summer.

S. uliginosa
Tall

Particularly useful as it is late flowering. Grows to 1.5m (5ft) with mid-blue spires. Moist soil and sheltered site.

Scabiosa
Scabiosa columbaria var. ochroleuca
Medium

A clump-forming perennial with grey-green leaves. A mass of wiry stems carry pale yellow pincushion flowers over a long period. Sun and a well-drained preferably limy soil preferred.

S. caucasia 'Clive Greaves'
Medium

Has blue flowers all summer, is reliable and does not need staking.

Sedum Herbstfreude (syn. 'Autumn Joy')
ICE-PLANT
Small

An excellent performer with oval jade green leaves and large flat flower heads comprising of small star-shaped pink flowers which are produced in late summer. The colour deepens to a coppery red turning brown in winter. The flower heads can be left over winter. Requires full sun and a rich well-drained soil.

Sisyrinchium striatum
Medium

Iris like evergreen leaves with spikes of cream flowers. Self-seeding. Variegated form named S.s. 'Aunt May' has same flower.

Sedum 'Herbstfreude' (syn. 'Autumn Joy')

Tiarella wherryi 'Bronze Beauty'
Small

A slow-growing perennial with reddish-brown toothed maple-shaped leaves. The dark stems carry pale pink starry flowers from early summer. The plant is shallow-rooting and requires a shady position in cool well-drained but rich soil. Not invasive.

Verbascum Cotswold Hybrid Group 'Gainsborough'
MULLEIN
Large

This semi-evergreen perennial has a basal rosette of crinkled grey green leaves which produce a tall branching spire covered in pale lemon yellow florets from early to late summer. Tolerates shade but prefers a sunny position with well-drained soil.

Viola cornuta 'Alba Minor'
Small

White flowers in early summer, sometimes re-occurs in late summer. Sun or semi-shade. V. 'Molly Sanderson' is a black-purple hybrid, with flowers throughout summer. Similar is V. 'Maggie Mott' which is pale blue. V. 'Moonlight' is pale yellow, from early to midsummer.

GRASSES

Carex
SEDGE

C. buchananii
LEATHERLEAF SEDGE GRASS

Reddish-brown attractive ever-green. Moist enriched soil.

C. elata 'Aurea'
BOWLES' GOLDEN SEDGE
Small

Arching leaves are yellow for much of the summer. Damp soil preferred but slow to establish.

C. 'Frosted Curls'
Small

Silver-green arching and curled leaves.

C. oshimensis 'Evergold' (syn. C. morrowii 'Evergold')

Small

Reliable evergreen with yellow and green striped leaves with a clump-forming habit.

Deschampsia cespitosa

TUFTED HAIR GRASS

Medium

Dense tussocks of elegantly slim leaves reaching 1.2m (4ft). Best in sunny sites where soils are preferably acidic and do not dry out. *D.c.* 'Bronze Veil' and *D.c.* 'Golden Dew' have particularly fine flower plumes and the latter is more compact.

Festuca

FESCUE

Small

F. glauca and *F. gautieri* (syn. *F. scoparia*) are both neat tufted grasses. The former is remarkably bluish and 25cm (10in) tall. The latter is a rich velvet green but denser and 20cm (8in) tall.

Milium effusum 'Aureum'

Small

An attractive butter yellow, this grass is fragile-looking but will grow in light shade. Not long-lived but does seed itself efficiently. Graceful yellow flowers reach 60cm (2ft) above much shorter foliage.

Miscanthus

SILVER GRASS

There are many good ornamental grasses in this genus. Clump-forming and good as windbreaks. Flowers best in hot summers.

M. sacchariflorus

Tall

A fast-growing grass which will reach 2.7m (9ft) by late summer. It is bluish-grey with long arching leaves, providing a rustling screen which, unlike many bamboos, is not invasive.

M. sinensis

Tall

Clump-forming graceful grasses which will grow in sun or shade and are tolerant of moist soils. *M. s.* 'Gracillimus' has elegantly slim leaves and reaches 1.5m (5ft). *M. s.* 'Silver Feather' is outstanding for the parchment-white sprays of flowers in late summer. *M. s.* 'Zebrinus' (porcupine grass) is cross-banded with yellow striped variegation and reaches 1.5m (5ft).

Pennisetum

FOUNTAIN GRASS

Tussocks are large and reliable. Arching narrow leaves. Some produce attractive flowers.

P. alopecuroides

AUSTRALIAN FOUNTAIN GRASS

Medium

Bright green with distinctive silver-brown panicles in late summer. The height is 90cm (3ft) or more and the parchment foliage will last through winter. Site in full sun. Fertile moist soil.

P. orientale

ORIENTAL FOUNTAIN GRASS

Small

This is a lighter green plant and is 45cm (18in) tall. The flowers are exceptional being a soft rose-grey and resembling fluffy caterpillars towards the end of summer. Full sun and well-drained, sandy soil.

Stipa

FEATHER GRASSS

Remarkable for their narrow leaves and attractive feathery flowers.

S. calamagrostis

Medium

A generously flowering grass with fine shimmering feathery sprays which arch over as they develop. Due to this it may need support.

S. gigantea

Tall

Magnificent grass carrying a shimmering haze of purplish oat-like flowers which are self-supporting. The height can be over 2m (6ft).

Milium effusum 'Aureum'

INDEX

Page references in *italics* are to captions and to planting plans

ACKNOWLEDGEMENTS

I am indebted to my friend Valerie Osmotherly for her untiring help, wisdom and cheerful support in the preparation of the text, and to the able assistance of my daughter Griselda Billington.

I would like to thank Clive Nichols for his patient and excellent photography, and I greatly appreciate the sensitive quality of the beautiful illustrations by Liz Petherall. Thanks are also due to Patrick McLeavy and Richard Carr, who designed the book with such care, and to Jane Birch for her thorough editing. Finally, I must add that without the inspiration of Lynn Bryan this book would not exist.

Grateful thanks are also due to those garden owners who generously allowed access to their gardens for photography: Mr and Mrs J. Brading; George Graham; Anthony Hanson; Mr and Mrs Manolis; Diana Stewart; and Mr and Mrs Keith Woolf.

I also appreciate those garden owners listed below who share their gardens through photography. Finally I must thank professional design colleagues, also listed below, whose work is shown in this book.

Jill Billington

PHOTOGRAPH ACKNOWLEDGEMENTS

Jacket: (front) Red Gables, Worcestershire/(back main picture) designer: Sue Berger, Bristol/(inset left) Longacre, Kent/(inset right) Hadspen House Garden and Nursery, Somerset; pp. 1 and 2–3 Eastgrove Cottage Garden, Sankyns Green, Worcestershire; p. 5 (top) Eastgrove Cottage Garden, Sankyns Green, Worcestershire; (bottom) Greenhurst, Sussex; p. 6 The Old Rectory, Sudborough, Northamptonshire; p. 8 Castle Howard, Yorkshire; p. 9 designer: Sue Berger, Bristol; p. 10 designer: Daniel Pearson; pp. 13 and 15 designer: Paula Rainey Crofts; p. 16 Coates Manor Garden, Sussex; p. 17 (bottom) Ramster, Surrey; p. 18 Cerney House, Gloucestershire; p. 19 (top) designer: Jill Billington/(bottom) The Manor House, Walton-in-Gordano, Avon; p. 20 designer: Eluned Price, Oxford; p. 21 Wolfson College, Oxford; pp. 22–3 Loreto Garden, Oxfordshire; p. 24 and 25 designer: Jill Billington; p. 27 Copton Ash, Kent; p. 28 designer: Nigel Colborn; p. 29 designer: Richard Coward; p. 30 40 Osler Road, Oxford; p. 31 The Priory, Kemerton, Worcestershire; pp. 32–3 RHS Garden, Wisley, Woking, Surrey; p. 35 designer: Sue Berger; p. 36 Ashtree Cottage, Wiltshire; p. 37 Hadspen House Garden and Nursery, Somerset; p. 38 Bear Ash, Berkshire; p. 39 The Anchorage, Kent; pp. 40–1 The Old Rectory, Sudborough, Northamptonshire; p. 43 Wollerton Old Hall, Shropshire; p. 44 Hadspen House Garden and Nursery, Somerset; p. 45 (top) The Anchorage, Kent/(bottom) designer: Jill Billington; p. 47 The Old Rectory, Sudborough, Northamptonshire; p. 48 Redenham Park, Hampshire/designer: Olivia Clarke; p. 49 Turn End Garden, Haddenham, Buckinghamshire; p. 50 (top) Little Coopers, Hampshire/(bottom) Longacre, Kent; pp. 51, 53 and 54 designer: Jill Billington; p. 55 Wolfson College Oxford; p. 56 (top) designer: Sheila Jackson; p. 57 Yew Tree Cottage, Sussex; p. 59 Little Coopers, Hampshire; pp. 60–1 Longacre, Kent; p. 62 Southview Nurseries, Hampshire; p. 63 Arley Hall, Cheshire; p. 66 (top and bottom) Herterton House, Northumberland; p. 67 designer: Jill Billington; pp. 68–9 The Priory, Kemerton, Worcestershire; p. 70 Turn End Garden, Haddenham, Hampshire; p. 71 (top) Brook Cottage, Oxfordshire/(bottom)

The Old Rectory, Sudborough, Northamptonshire; p. 72 Turn End Garden, Haddenham, Buckinghamshire; p. 73 Copton Ash, Kent; p. 74 The Anchorage, Kent; p. 75 Crathes Castle, Scotland; p. 76 Eastgrove Cottage Garden, Sankyns Green, Worcestershire; p. 77 (top) The Priory, Kemerton, Worcestershire/(bottom) Hadspen House Garden and Nursery, Somerset; p. 78 Turn End Garden, Haddenham, Buckinghamshire; p. 80 The Old Rectory, Burghfield, Berkshire; p. 82 designer: Anthony Noel; p. 83 The Old School House, Essex; p. 84 The Chipping Croft, Gloucestershire; p. 86 Red Gables, Worcestershire; p. 87 The Priory, Kemerton, Worcestershire; p. 88 (top) designer: Nigel Colborn/(bottom) Tintinhull House and Garden, Somerset, owned by the National Trust; p. 89 (top) designer: Anthony Noel; p. 90 Hadspen House Garden and Nursery, Somerset; p. 91 designer: Paula Rainey Crofts; p. 92: designer: Jo Passmore; p. 93 (left) designer: Jill Billington/(right) designer: Joan Murdy; p. 96 designer: Mark Brown; p. 97 The Beth Chatto Gardens, Elmstead Market, Essex; p. 98 Hadspen House Garden and Nursery, Somerset; p. 100 Longacre, Kent; p. 101 (top) Little Coopers, Hampshire/(bottom) designer: Jill Billington; p. 102 The Beth Chatto Gardens, Elmstead Market, Essex; p. 103 Brook Cottage, Oxfordshire; p. 106 Southview Nurseries, Hampshire; p. 107 designer: Jill Billington; p. 108 The Beth Chatto Gardens, Elmstead Market, Essex; p. 109 Olivers, Essex; p. 111 40 Osler Road, Oxford; pp. 112–13 Spinners Nursery, Hampshire; p. 115 Little Coopers, Hampshire; p. 117 Spinners Nursery, Hampshire; p. 119 Southview Nurseries, Hampshire; p. 120 Hadspen House Garden and Nursery, Somerset; p. 121 designers: Mathew Bell and Nuala Hancock; p. 122 (top) The Anchorage, Kent; p. 123 Cerney House, Gloucestershire; p. 124 The Anchorage, Kent; p. 125 The Manoir Aux Quat Saisons, Oxfordshire; p. 126 Sticky Wicket, Buckland Newton, Dorset; p. 127 Hadspen House Garden and Nursery, Somerset; p. 129 Bide-A-Wee Cottage, Northumberland; p. 131 (left) Chenies Manor House, Rickmansworth, Buckinghamshire; p. 134 Hadspen House Garden and Nursery, Somerset.